Manipulation & Dark Psychology Protection Blueprint: The Truth About Dark Persuasion, NLP, Body Language & How To Analyze People Techniques & How You Can Protect Against Them

By Unlimited Potential Publications

TABLE of CONTENTS

Introduction 10

Chapter 1 – Mind Control Through the Ages 17

Mind Manipulation in Rome (Classical and Later)....17

Behaviorism – The Scientific Basis of Mind Manipulation 23

Mind Manipulation of the Masses: Mussolini and Hitler 25

Mind Manipulation Experiments in Nazi Concentration Camps 26

The 1950s: Hollywood and Manipulative Commercials 27

The CIA's Declassified Mind Control Program: Project Bluebird and MKUltra 31

The Weaponization of Mind Control Techniques and Technology 33

The Rise of Social Media and Mind Manipulation....34

Key Elements of Mind Manipulation 36

Chapter 2 – The Subconscious 38

The Strange Case of Seb and the E-Cigarette 38

The Subconscious Exists, and We "Do Things" when We are Subconscious... 40

What Is the Subconscious?....................................... 41

Conscious, Subconscious and Unconscious Mind 43

How to Manipulate the Subconscious...................... 44

How to Access the Subconscious.............................. 45

Cultural Factors and the Manipulation of the Subconscious 48

The First Step against Mind Manipulation 51

Levels of Alertness in the Conscious Mind 54

Activities and Substances that Raise Alertness 58

Bypassing the Conscious Mind 59

Chapter 3 – Training Your Conscious Mind............... 62

Increase Your Basic Attention and Awareness Levels 63

What Does It Mean "to Be Aware"?.......................... 64

Activities That Increase Your Conscious Awareness Levels 66

Sports – Especially Team Sports 67

Strolling 68

Martial Arts 69

Meditation... 70

Visiting Parks and Other Natural Places............. 71

Mindfulness 72

Eating Slowly 73

Painting and Other Arts...................................... 73

Gardening... 74

Chapter 4 – Signs and Symptoms of Mind Manipulation **75**

The Difference between Signs and Symptoms of Mind Manipulation 76

Spotting Signs of Mind Manipulation 77

Repetition 78

Doublespeak 79

Over-Emphatic Language.. 80

Empty Claims and Incorrect Use of Data 81

Insistence and Aggressiveness................................... 84

Linking Unrelated Things, Images, Thoughts............ 85

Body Language.. 85

Talking too Fast.. 87

Elusiveness.. 87

Symptoms of Mind Manipulation.............................. 90

Cravings and Unhealthy Interest in Something........ 91

Symptoms of Serious and Advanced Mind Manipulation 92

Chapter 5 – Behaviorism, Positive and Negative Reinforcement.. 99

Positive Reinforcement 100

Using Positive Reinforcement Correctly and Ethically 103

Negative Reinforcement... 107

Uses of Negative Reinforcement............................. 110

The Trap: Positive and Negative Reinforcements Together 112

Social Negative Reinforcement 115

Chapter 6 – Replacement Therapy for Mind Manipulation..117

What Is Replacement Therapy 118

Mind Manipulation & Replacement Therapy 120

Replacement Therapy Must Be Enjoyable.............. 122

Add Extra Rewards to the Replacement................. 126

Planning and Structuring Replacement Therapy.... 127

Choose the time to start well 128

Don't expect too much too soon 128

Be flexible 128

Don't beat yourself up if things go wrong....... 129

Start with about 5 to 10%, not more! 130

Add extra rewards at each stage 131

Involve others 131

Reflect regularly 132

What's inside a word? 133

Chapter 7 – Neuro Linguistic Programming (NLP) 134

Does NLP Work? 135

Developments in NLP 137

Applications of NLP... 137

Anchoring.. 139

Belief Change 140

Reframing Content: Rephrase and Reformulate Sentences.. 144

Mirroring... 145

Synonyms Matter 147

Visualization and Metaphor 149

The Bright Side of NLP 151

How to Use NLP for Good Reasons........................ 153

Getting Personal 155

Chapter 8 – Manipulators in Everyday Life.............156

What Turns People into Manipulators 156

How to Spot the "Manipulator among Us" 159

Psychopaths and Sociopaths 163

Dealing with Everyday Life Manipulators.............. 166

Find Out What They Want..................................... 167

Give Conflicting Signals.. 168

Don't Reward Flattery 171

Ignore the Manipulator as Much as Possible 172

Avoid Any Type of Confrontation with the Manipulator 173

Get the Manipulator to Understand You Know What Sort of Person S/He Is.. 174

Involve Significant Others and Get Their Viewpoint 174

Don't Give the Manipulator Any Money 175

From Skinner's Box to "the Box" 176

Chapter 9 – Mind Manipulation on Television.........177

TV News and "Spin" 177

An Alternative to TV News.................................... 182

TV and Social Media 183

The Quality of TV Programs.................................... 184

Cutting Down on Time in Front of the TV.............. 186

TV Commercials 187

Television and Alpha Waves.................................... 189

Cut Down on Television Time... 192

Chapter 10 – The Professional Salesperson 194

From Old Fashioned Door to Door Salespeople to Today's Professionals 195

Look at Their Eyes.. 197

Don't Let Them into Your Home and Keep them in an Emotionally Neutral Place 199

Elude Questions.. 200

Keep Them at a Physical Distance 201

Be "Cruel" with Your Handshake............................ 202

Demotivate the Manipulator................................... 203

Kick It into the Long Grass 204

Ask for a Written Document, Agreement or Contract 206

Don't Allow Manipulators to Hurry You When Reading a Document 208

Don't Lad Them On...209

Chapter 11 – Social Media: The Last Frontier of Mass Manipulation...212

How Social Media Isolates You...............................213

Internet and Social Media Bubbles.........................216

Social Media and Behaviorism................................219

Fake News on Social Media 221

How to Fact Check Fake News................................222

Primary and Secondary Sources 224

Look for Consistency...227

Expect Correctness 229

Understand Bias...231

Fake Accounts..234

What's in a Word? The Language of Social Media . 240

The Two Faces of Social Media...............................243

Chapter 12 – Deconditioning and Rewiring Your Brain and Mind..246

Understand Natural Time Cycles 247

Drugs and Brain Wiring..253

Can You Rewire Your Brain without Psychedelic Drugs?
....255

Choose the Best Timing 256

Don't Let Fear Dominate You 258

Prepare for Bed..259

Find a "Switch off Time" 261

Rewiring Is Like Training 263

Mind Your Diet.. 265

Keep Your Brain Fit!... 267

Mens Sana in Corpore Sano................................... 268

Choose a Positive Setting for Your Rewiring 268

Do Meditation.. 270

Use Music to Rewire Your Brain 271

While you are doing the exercises:......................... 272

Chapter 13 – Exercises to Rewire Your Brain 273

Belly Breathing... 273

Draw Your Dreams... 275

Smell Flowers... 275

Flip Your Conditioned Behaviors 276

Mind Your Language... 277

Use Positive Language 278

Use Positive Affirmations 279

Use Visualization.. 281

Laugh! 283

Conclusion..285

Reference Page..289

Introduction

Have you ever walked out of a shop with something you didn't really want? Maybe you only realized it later, but still... Have you ever looked back on a vote you cast, even years later and thought, "That wasn't really wise at all!" Or have you ever done something, at work for example, that turned out to be against your own interests? Well, you are not alone!

More and more, especially with the advent of social media, people are finding out far too late that they are being manipulated constantly. The Cambridge Analytica case is a flagrant example of how it is possible to change enough people's minds long enough (two days before the voting in this case) to get the election results you want. Whichever side you are on the vote in question, what interests us is the idea, now proven, that manipulation exists, it is being used, and we need to defend ourselves from it.

In fact, manipulation is one of the oldest psychological practices in the world. You see, while Sigmund Freud was creating that basis of psychoanalysis, and tried to free people from mental problems, at that very time someone else,

Pavlov, was teaching the world that **mind manipulation and conditioning is real, easy, and feasible!**

How many ads have you seen in your life? Well, I'll leave the exact math to you, but only on TV, we are exposed to 40,000 ads a year! This is according to data found by the *Pediatrics,* Dec. 2006, in a study called 'Children, Adolescents, and Advertising' written by the American Academy of Pediatrics. And this is for children, adults may well be exposed to more!

Advertising is a $250 billion a year industry; surely they would not spend this money year on year if they didn't get something in return... And they do! On average, they get almost 10 times as much back...

"But what is advertising, and where does advertising end," you may ask? Good question... Now experts talk of *"marketing"* and *"targeting".* I personally feel insulted at least, threatened even to know that for business I am a "target". But your question goes deeper, doesn't it?

The line between what is at least "explicit" advertising and "covert" advertising has been blurred for decades now. A star wearing a particular brand of sneakers is most likely advertising. Have you not noticed how rappers and R&B always put their sneakers in clear view? Was James Dean publicizing cigarette smoking? Did Chanel make money out of Marilyn Monroe's famous statement that she only wore #5 in bed?

Sometimes these people don't even know that they are conditioning your mind, selling a product. For example, I suspect James Dean was unaware of the fact that he made cigarettes so cool that a whole generation felt "nerdy" or "uncool" unless they smoked… And surely, he was not "the only part of the mind conditioning machine". Even medical doctors were fooled into promoting what is in fact "rolled up poison" … But this again shows how it is possible to condition a whole generation.

But once we go past the explicit/covert line, is there more? I bet there is. Secret services have been working mind conditioning for decades. The famous case of MK Ultra, the officially acknowledged mind control program of the CIA experimented on citizens from 1953 to 1973 (officially…) In this time, they managed to experiment all sorts of mind control techniques, including using heavy drugs, and they did it on unwitting US and Canadian citizens… Yes, they experimented on people without them even knowing about it (which is very unethical).

In serious cases, *mind manipulation leads to becoming dysfunctional or totally nonfunctional in*

society. People who have been serious victims often lose their job, social standing, even friends! Now, these are critical cases, but to a small extent, any level of mind manipulation interferes with your proficiency at work, with your social life, and even with your relationships.

Ok, now I see you are getting worried. I just wanted to show you how *real, widespread, multifaceted, and well documented mind manipulation is,* and that it has many levels. But of course, **I am here to give you a solution to mind manipulation!**

Let me tell you: everybody is under *some level of mind manipulation.* And in my professional life, I have even had to work on freeing people from mind conditioning. Mind conditioning is a more serious case than mind manipulation. It too happens at many levels and in many forms, but it's like addiction. You have to do something, but you don't understand why.

The good news is that **stopping mind control on you means taking control of your life.** And it is even more effective if you take family and/or friends with you on this liberating journey!

But for most readers, I suppose the main worry will be a low to medium level of mind manipulation. That is very common nowadays. But how can you get out of it?

Well, first of all you need to **know and recognize mind manipulation channels and techniques.** And you will! Just read on and in the very first few chapters of this book you will find an in-depth, detailed but easily explained analysis of all these. We will also do it in a practical way, with exercises. And I apologize in advance if, even at the early stages of "analysis" I won't resist giving some solutions.

We will of course also look at many **techniques to protect yourself from mind manipulation, and even to deprogram your mind.** The mind, you see, can be wired or unwired to a certain response. Put in the simplest possible way, mind manipulation wires your mind so that it gives a specific response. A whole mental disorder has been "invented and inflicted on people" *compulsive buying disorder,* which is how psychologists refer to "shopaholics".

In the same way as you can unwire your mind from seeking a solution in alcohol or drugs, so can you for other manipulations. But of course, it also means changing your life habits... You won't cure an alcoholic by getting him or her to work in a wine bar (even worse a wine cellar).

I know that changing habits is always met with, "Mmmm, not sure I want to change my life; I'm quite comfortable with it..." But I promise you that it will actually be fun. Most of the mind manipulation channels, activities and outlets are actually boring, and you can replace them with something far better. We will look at that too.

And we will even look at serious cases, of course. But in all this, I promise you that we will keep the tone light, but I will always be professional. And we will go through many concepts and solutions, and quick tricks to protect yourself and also many easy, short but when possible fun exercises too.

So, think about it for a second. Do you really want to continue being a victim of manipulation? Every day under mind manipulation is a day you miss out on freedom and real life. And trust me, life is so much better without it! In fact, ***taking action against low-level and high-level mind manipulation means taking back control over your life!***

The sooner you start, the sooner you will actually be free. And – trust me – your social, personal, romantic, and professional life will be so much better! You will even *sleep better!*

And let me tell you what the first step to fight mind manipulation is: decide to get out of it... So now you do have the choice: you can choose to read on and soon be free... Will you?

If you now feel like a cog in an inhumane machine, reading this book is like opening a door to a garden of freedom, the garden of your real self and real potential... And I'd like to show you how to open this door, get rid of the old manipulated "cog life" and bloom as you are meant to...

Shall we start now?

Chapter 1 – Mind Control Through the Ages

I want to tell you a story. A story that is not told. Actually, it is the same story you learn at school, but from another perspective... Let me take it from an artistic point of view – why not? Maybe at school you studied art history, or you just like visiting art galleries, museums, and beautiful architectural buildings like churches...

Mind Manipulation in Rome (Classical and Later)

Walk into an old church, like those you find at every street corner in Europe. Ok, what do you see? You will say, "I can see beautiful columns, a great decorative altar, and lots of statues, paintings and art on the walls." I agree, that's what you see, but you can see more... Look at those paintings, why do you think so much time, effort, talent, and money was spent on them? They are not just there to decorate the place...

They are there to tell stories to people. Often people who could not read, and often stories they could not fully understand. True, our culture has changed and things that were clear once, are now harder to understand. But the deep meaning of many paintings, like Michelangelo's fresco on the Sistine Chapel's ceiling, in the Vatican, Rome is still debated by top academics and art historians all over the world. Do you think the average farmer would really understand the deep meanings of such art?

But did it matter though that the peasant understood the narrative and deeper meaning of those stories? No, it didn't. Exactly like it does not matter if you follow an ad on TV or you turn to something else… **It's the impression that matters.**

Some architectural styles like Baroque were literally invented to manipulate the minds of common people. It was literally devised to give an impression of grandeur, opulence, but also of strength and control, over nature and over society. So, if you lived in Rome or Sicily in the Seventeenth Century, it did not matter if you understood all the symbolism etc. of those impressive buildings… What mattered was that you walked away convinced that the Roman Catholic Church, not the reformed church, was in charge, over you and over nature.

Think about it, most of what remains in history is the product of mind manipulation attempts. The Colosseum, not to go too far, but to step 15 centuries back in history, was a colossal (excuse me the pun) but **very conscious attempt at controlling people's minds and behavior.**

It is well known that the Roman elite paid for and offered grueling and violent shows to "the people" (by which we mean everybody, not just citizens) in order to control them. You see, if you are angry and you project your anger against a gladiator, or someone being mauled and eaten alive by lions, well, then you walk away "satisfied" – *and you won't release that anger against the "government", the emperor, and the imperial institutions.*

This was done with purpose and very consciously, both by the Pope (in the first case) and by all emperors and the aristocracy (the ruling class) of Rome. And we can already get one key point: **mind manipulation has been consistently and regularly used throughout history, even on a massive scale.**

"When did mind manipulation start," is a common question. The answer is that we don't know exactly, but we can see traces of it in ancient civilizations. Kings being depicted as superior, even "superhumans" is a sign of it. For sure by the Golden Age of Rome, it was in full swing, and used on a colossal scale.

The Birth of Scientific Mind Manipulation in the Nineteenth Century

However, *mind manipulation in ancient times was rational, effective, and even well designed but not "scientific".* The Romans understood human behavior, and they acted upon it to get the desired reaction from people. In their history, causing wars, prompting the enemy to attack first etc. were common and well devised tactics. In fact, even nowadays we use the Latin (Roman) phrase *"casus belli"* (a reason for war); they caused the reason, then blamed their enemies for starting the war... And we still do it!

But what I was saying is that we cannot call it "scientific" for two reasons: at the time science as we know it technically did not exist; it was not so much based on data and analysis, more on "reason and intuition". At least as far as we know. *Modern mind manipulation instead is scientific.* And that makes it even worse because:

- *It is more effective (powerful).*

- *It is more hidden, less detectable and more "obscure".*

It is, in a few words, much more subtle, but also much more pervasive... We will see very soon how it works… You need to know it to avoid it, of course. But when did it become scientific then?

It was somewhere towards the end of the Nineteenth Century that the full scientific grounds of mind manipulation were laid. But, like with all scientific advancements, or at least most, there was "something in the air already" before the actual breakthrough was made.

In our case, what was "in the air was smog" … Are you puzzled? I am trying to… You see, during the Industrial Revolution, mass production was invented and developed in England and the UK. London is filled with smog, but the market is filled with products…

Unlike what was happening before, these products had to be placed. In a society where little changes for generations, like a typical pre-industrial society, people know what they need, and they buy what they have known to work for them.

But if you are producing more, and new things, you need to find a way to convince them that they need your product. You see the problem? So, Victorian England saw the birth of advertising…

Advertising is, at its most honest and explicit level, quite acceptable. It can be seen as "information". But look at where it has gone, and in many cases the only actual information you get is the name of the product and, in some cases, that quick sentence at the end warning you about side effects!

Like with many things we will see in this book, ***the line between "explicit and honest" to "hidden and dishonest"*** gets blurred and then problems start. At first, advertisements were basic drawings of the product with name and price. Then the motto came, and then more and more sophisticated ways of "convincing you to buy" came about...

In Victorian times, from what I have studied, advertising remained mostly honest, if at times pushy. It was still on the side of "informing and trying to convince" rather than "manipulating". But soon things changed.

It was in fact towards the end of the Victorian Era (1837 – 1901) that two "scientists of the mind" were making great discoveries... And we have met them already: the Austrian **Sigmund Freud**, the "Father of Psychoanalysis" as everybody calls him and the Russian **Ivan Pavlov**, the "Father of Behaviorism", as he is called, but also the "father of mind control" as he is called behind closed doors.

We will come back to Freud in more detail in the next chapter because it is thanks to some of his studies, especially on ***the subconscious*** that on the one hand, mind control and manipulation have become more effective and powerful, on the other hand, **understanding how the subconscious works leads us to the solution to mind manipulation and control.**

Behaviorism – The Scientific Basis of Mind Manipulation

As for **Behaviorism**, we need to talk about it right now. **Behaviorism is at the core of all mind manipulation and mind control techniques.** Pavlov was a psychologist and he even won the Nobel Prize for his work. He did research in involuntary reflex actions but especially in **conditioning**.

Famous is his experiment of the dog and the bell. He would ring a bell every time he would give the dog some food. When we say, "Pavlov's dog," however, we mean "dogs" because he used more than 40, Bierka, Beck, Ika, Joy – ok, I'm not going to list them all... The dogs would salivate every time they saw the food. And they ended up associating the bell with food. Pavlov then stopped giving them food, and you know what? The dogs kept salivating every time they heard the bell even without food.

This method is at the basis of modern dog training, but also of much education for Humans, where we associate academic success with pleasure and failure with pain (emotional, but in the past physical too...) and it is also behind much of our behavior even when at work...

Watson and Rayner: The Development of Mind Conditioning – A Tribute to Little Albert

To be honest, it was *John B. Watson, another behaviorist who discovered the full power of fear in mind conditioning.* The experiments he carried out with his graduate student *Rosalie Rayner* just before 1920 were cruel to start with. He used a child, a baby, whose name will go down in history as the first Human martyr of mind conditioning: *Little Albert.*

They gave Little Albert some things he had never seen, like a rat, a monkey, a mask etc. They called these *stimuli* (mark this word, we'll use it a lot). The baby was fine with all of them. Then, every time poor Little Albert touched the rat, they produced a very scary and upsetting noise. No need to say that when they showed the rat, even without the noise, to Little Albert again, he was frightened… Basically they caused a phobia in a child in the name of science…

The fact is that this system then became the core of education all over the world, and physical punishment, which already was in use, now had a "scientific justification". Ok, one of the sinister consequences of the "Little Albert Experiment" was many aching knuckles and even buttocks…

The other, however, is that ***mind conditioning and mind manipulation started to refine the use of reward and punishment associated with a stimulus to become more and more powerful and effective.*** If you have seen *Clockwise Orange* by Stanley Kubrick, you may think that it was all fiction...

No... What you see in the film is actually very mild compared to what mind control experiments would become in about three to four decades from where we left our story, and we'll get there soon... in 1920 Watson and Rayner published their study...

Mind Manipulation of the Masses: Mussolini and Hitler

In 1922 another event showed the power of mind control, not on a baby, not on an individual, but on a whole country: Mussolini rose to power. What? Mussolini? Yes, Mussolini is arguably the most dangerous and imitated dictator in modern times, more than Hitler in some respects. He was not as cruel, but he worked out one thing: ***control the most modern means of communication and you can get a whole country to do as you wish.***

This happened near the time of the peak of technological progress (1930 ca. it has been slowing down ever since), and this is the formula all dictators and wannabe tyrants have used since.

Mussolini, thanks to Marconi, understood the power of the radio, took control of it, and used it to:

- **Convince enough people to back him up on the way to power.**

- **Stop any form of dissent and create a false perception of reality once in power.**

Eleven years later Hitler did exactly the same, just with a more modern communication system: the television...

So, we went into World War II, the most horrible conflict in the history of the whole world because two people, very keen on behaviorism – both of them – managed to control the instruments necessary to manipulate the minds of entire populations...

Mind Manipulation Experiments in Nazi Concentration Camps

During this horrible war, the Nazis carried out mind control experiments in Auschwitz and Dachau concentration camps. The experiments were first realized in Auschwitz then repeated for confirmation in Dachau. No need to say that they were horrible and unethical; the idea was to reduce people to animals, machines, or slaves.

They used drugs, in particular peyote, and of course, they did not go down the "positive conditioning" route, but the negative one, using fear and torture to control people's minds and bend (actually annihilate) their will. Luckily their experiments concluded that "mescaline was too unreliable" for mind control.

What happened, however, as Professor David Salinas Flores presents in *SM Physical Medicine and Rehabilitation,* Dec 28, 2018, 'Mind Control: from Nazis to DAPRA', a review of how a particular time in the history of mind control, where the transition from Nazi to CIA led experiments took place – what happened, I was saying, is that the CIA got hold of the papers written by Dr Kurt Plönter, the SS physician that led the experiments.

And no, they did not sleep on them. But we will come to the CIA in a minute, as they are the "big experimenters" when it comes to the (at the time) hidden history of mind control and manipulation, I mean, the one they really tried to conceal...

The 1950s: Hollywood and Manipulative Commercials

But there is the other thread in our story: that mind control which occurs under everybody's eyes... So, what happened after WWII? So far, we have seen that first it was paintings and maybe hymns, then the radio, then television. In the 50s the big medium of communication was the "moving pictures" or the cinema.

During the 1950s we saw Hollywood rise to its maximum splendor, promoting, on the one side, the great Hollywood stars we remember with fondness still nowadays. On the other, it also promoted a world view; it was, quite clearly, trying to manipulate the masses.

The idea that you need to fight a faraway enemy, the American dream, the idea that the middle-class household and life was the only possible pursuit for average people... All these were promoted... You see, selling a dream and selling a nightmare at the same time is a way of manipulating minds. So, Hollywood told us that "out there" there was a horrible and cruel enemy, and when that enemy disappeared (the end of the USSR), they just replaced it with others.

They also depicted "internal enemies": Native Americans in Western movies and then – well how many Black villains can you see in movies? Far too many.

On the other side, the happy family, mostly rural or suburban, with traditional values, with a severe but benign father who goes out to work and a mother who stays at home and whose only ambition is to clean the kitchen was presented as a dream...

They do adapt dreams and nightmares, don't worry. But they will still keep you in this *"punishment / reward" pattern, which is at the core of Behaviorism and mind control.* You see, movies, radio programs, tv shows etc., are all *stimuli*.

As are advertisements! Look at the now classical ads of the 1950s and you will see that they too are telling this Hollywood story, but they add an element: you need to *buy* to be happy. So, the wife is not so happy about cleaning the kitchen, but "having the new vacuum cleaner to clean it" ...

A massive operation of mind manipulation started in the 1950s: it was aimed to turn people into consumers, and they succeeded, giving birth to that phenomenon that is consumerism, and we now are at a pathological stage of this "collective syndrome".

You see how it took time, yes, but with insistence, while before you would look for happiness in peace, relationships, etc., we now look for it primarily in gadgets and social media interactions. Not only, in most cases (in quite a few yes, however), but in the vast majority of people far too much anyway. That all started in the 50s

There is a famous and interesting episode here. That was the time when the USA was becoming "urban and modern" and ready-made products were starting to flood the market. You see, before that time, you would cook everything from the base ingredients. Betty Crocker Cake Mixes came on the market. It was perfect: you just needed to mix it and the dough was ready... But no one liked it. It was meant to be a great success... But it wasn't.

So, what was the problem? They did what was at those times a very modern market research and they found out that women wanted to have modern conveniences, but they still wanted to see themselves as "angels of the hearth", as "traditional" and capable of cooking... So, they just added a hand with two eggs to the commercial, and the slogan "Betty Crocker Cake Mixes bring you that Special Homemade Goodness" and "Because you add the eggs yourself." And it was a huge success.

Thing is, they found a weak spot in the psychology of a group of people which is that they wanted to fool themselves, because the whole story that you buy a mix and then buy eggs and that it's a "homemade" cake is hardly believable, is it? But this shows how subtle mind control was becoming...

The CIA's Declassified Mind Control Program: Project Bluebird and MKUltra

But the 50s did not hold back on the occult experiments on mind control either. Actually, they reached a peak. In this decade the CIA launched Project **Bluebird** in 1951, and the already mentioned **MKUltra** in 1953. Do you remember the SS Doctor who experimented in concentration camps? Well apparently, he even received help from the West, yes, from their sworn enemies, and his studies ended up becoming the groundwork for MKUltra.

And if what they did does not make good and easy reading: they experimented **hallucinogenic drugs like LSD on behavior modification** (which is an established byword for mind manipulation). And the numbers read are frightening:

- Scientists from 80 worldwide renowned institution
- 12 hospitals
- 44 schools
- 149 sub-projects

All these were being hidden from the people and were studying various aspects of mind control techniques. And these included:

- **_Controlling brain activity;_** they studied how you can "wire and rewire" the brain by promoting and discouraging the formation of neurons with positive and negative stimuli.

- **_Mind torture;_** they exposed people to horrible stimuli, in order to break their mind, when under the effects of LSD. They caused permanent damage to people's minds, and in 1963 they also used LSD on children (!!!) with mental problems, at times keeping them under the effects of LSD for months! This is a clear crime against Humanity, but it shows how far they were ready to go to pursue mind manipulation.

- **_Extortion;_** they used mapping of the brain with nanobots and managed to extract information that patients were keeping to themselves, and then forced them to do what they ordered them to do under blackmail.

As you can see, they used very advanced technology, like implants, nanobots, microchips and what is known as cerebral internet (a network of chips and nanobots within the brain). It sounds like science fiction; it is all recorded, documented and now declassified.

Take a long breath, take a pause... I understand that finding out about these appalling experiments can be disturbing... But there is worse...

The Weaponization of Mind Control Techniques and Technology

These experiments allegedly stopped in 1964, but the usually well informed say that of course they closed a program to open a new one, also because MKUltra was starting to "leak" to the press and – above all – to the People anyway...

But what we know for sure is that these experiments did not remain such: the results were then transferred to DAPRA, or Defense Advanced Research Project Agency, which developed actual weapons. Nowadays, the UN itself is investigating actual **weapons of mind control** in use in the USA.

These are called "non-lethal weapons" and they are not all aimed at mind manipulation, but some are, in particular **V2K (Voice to Skull).** This is no "conspiracy theory" as there have been court cases (more than 300) about its use on citizens, and all ended with compensation being imposed by the court for its use. And of course, the UN is investigating it. But what is more, the US Defense Dept openly admits its existence and use.

There is a letter from the Department of the Army, United States Intelligence and Security Command, Dec 13 2006, in response to a subject freedom of information request which clearly states that this is in use in the USA, details its effects on victims, causing "aural bioeffects" … This means that people "hear voices" that don't actually exist.

They use very "radiofrequency directed energy" (radio waves) to make people hear and see things that do not exist. They basically induce hallucinations in people's minds. And of course the victims, called "targeted individuals" (or TI's) have no idea what is going on, and in many cases they see it as a form of torture…

The letter now regards the information on this weapon of mind manipulation "declassified" but only with information up to 17 February 1998.

Who knows what happened next?

Take another deep breath, take another pause. This is the worst use of mind manipulation we officially know of… But the levels we have gotten to are chilling.

The Rise of Social Media and Mind Manipulation

Now back to the more "overt" side of our story. Mind control and mass manipulation – not the experiments on a few but the daily practice of the media…

Let's recap again, from paintings and songs to the radio, television and movies, and with the new "variant" in it, *advertising*, which is what *has made mind manipulation immediately profitable.* What has changed since the 1950s?

The most glaring difference is that now we have the internet and social media. And it is very topical now to talk about how social media are manipulating our minds. In fact, we will dedicate a whole chapter to them. Because *social media* have some very weird characteristics:

- *They isolate you from others:* this makes you more vulnerable to mind manipulation.

- *They are very quick and full of stimuli (with quick rewards like thumbs up or little hearts etc.)* Any psychologist can see that they are designed along behaviorist lines and that they are clearly designed to manipulate your mind.

- *They are available all day long now.* This is really dangerous. We moved from being exposed to mind conditioning a few times during the week, to every night, to a few hours a day, to all day and all week, from when we wake up to when we fall asleep.

And this leads us to what scientists call "the state of the art", which means "how things are at the moment". On the one hand, hidden (but then declassified) *studies on mind manipulation have used the most atrocious and inhumane techniques possible.* They have been kept hidden from view, and applied against people's will. Ok, it's hard to get someone's consent to be mentally manipulated, but it does not matter. It is unethical to experiment without consent, even more to cause damage to people without consent, even more to torture people, anyway.

On the other hand, *"low level", diffuse and not hidden mind manipulation has become more and more pervasive, powerful, and even invasive in our lives.* These are the two threads of the story so far.

Key Elements of Mind Manipulation

But we can already draw some conclusions, just from the history of mind manipulation (in modern times). Mind manipulation has some *key elements:*

- *The use of communication media;* the more powerful the medium, the more effective the mind manipulation.

- **A *hidden motivation;*** this is ***profit*** in the vast majority of cases, but extortion, espionage and making "enemies" non-functional are common motives for the more serious cases, even political adversaries can be targets, and often are.

- ***It uses Behaviorism;*** "targets" (as they call us) are given ***repeated stimuli*** followed by ***positive feedback*** for the response they want from us and ***negative feedback*** for responses they want to discourage. ***This is how they "rewire" our brain, i.e., and condition it to do what they want.***

Well, not bad. You already know the history of this field (I did concentrate on modern times; it's more relevant and we know more about it). But you now also know the basic workings of mind manipulation, the basic science behind it and its basic techniques. We will see them in detail in future chapters, of course, and we will, naturally ***learn many ways to prevent, slow down, block manipulation, and even to decondition and "rewire" your mind.*** But next I'm going to take you into a very surreal world, a world, a bit like a painting by Salvador Dalì... The world of the subconscious...

Chapter 2 – The Subconscious

The Strange Case of Seb and the E-Cigarette

Seb is a great friend of mine. Yesterday he told me a story he thought was strange... Guess what, it wasn't to me, but let me tell you, maybe you will disagree...

First let me give you some background information. Seb (Sebastian, of course) is 35, he has a good degree in biology. He is a very rational person, with a high IQ and a successful job and life. He does not drink in excess and he does not take drugs. He used to smoke, though. But he is giving up...

Like most people who give up smoking nowadays, he is using what is in fact replacement therapy, only a very fashionable one: vaping. It is in fact by far the most successful replacement therapy for smoking ever. You know that e-cigs can be fairly expensive and trendy, and that "vapers" now are so specialized and even "geeky" about them... anyway, he just got a new one through the mail yesterday, because, apparently, it's best to buy them online...

He got it, and he was very proud of it. He showed it to me; I must admit it looks great, with a colorful display and even a cool look... The fact is that he had been waiting for it for a few days. The old one was broken, and he gets a bit nervous, he even gets cravings for cigarettes still, if he does not vape... But he got it... He went out with it to try it out...

He got home, and you know what? The e-cig was gone! Gone! Vanished! Not on him anymore! So, he thought he'd dropped it... He went back and did the stressful thing of retracing his steps. Exactly and all... He has a good memory anyway... He looked everywhere but he couldn't find it anywhere...

Then he passed by a baker where he had stopped to buy a bun... And a man came out and said, "Are you looking for something?" He was taken aback, because he couldn't possibly have dropped it on that tiled floor... I mean, the noise alone... Anyway, he said, "Yes, my e-cig, it looks –"and the man stopped him... "Yes, we know," he said, "you put it on the counter and walked off; we even called after you, but you didn't respond..." and he handed Seb the e-cig back...

"Now, how is it possible that I put my e-cig on the counter? What for," was asking Seb when he saw me that night. You see, for him, he couldn't possibly have done it and, above all **he did not remember doing it**. Not at all! Even trying to remember – nothing! So, what happened?

The Subconscious Exists, and We "Do Things" when We are Subconscious

To me, the answer is simple: *he did not do it consciously, but subconsciously. Something in his mind made him do that action without him even being aware of it.* It happens, and it happens much more often than you may think.

We may speculate on what caused this "deviation" from normal behavior. *In many cases, stress can be the cause of these events.* Mark these words, because we are going to come back to them! So, maybe the stress of waiting for the e-cig, or work-related stress etc. But I didn't pry too much, so, for the time being, we cannot make a full diagnosis.

But I needed this example to show you that *we have subconscious behavior, and that it is not at all uncommon.* If *stress can cause it when unexpected and unwanted, unconscious behavior is actually very common in routine actions.*

Do you drive? Can you remember all the driving operations (pressing down on clutch, accelerator, brake, changing gear, turning left, right, using indicators, reading road signs etc....) from the last time you got home from work or school or college? Or even the stores? No, of course you can't! And the reason is simple, *all these actions, especially common and repeated ones, happen "under the radar of our Consciousness".*

When was the last time you forgot your keys? Why do you forget them? Or better, do you usually remember when you pick them up? No, of course you don't. You do lots of things mechanically. You do things and you are not actually conscious that you are doing them!

It happens to everybody, all the time, and at a very "low level", especially with common and repeated actions. We will see how *social media takes advantage of repeated actions to send things, including instructions on how to behave, into our subconscious*. But for now, think twice next time you put a "like" to a post, that they are actually giving you *stimuli* to respond to, like Pavlov's dogs, or a mouse in a maze...

What Is the Subconscious?

Yet, for the time being, we need to focus on the **concept of subconscious.** So far, we can say that *not all our mind is conscious, and that there is an area which is subconscious.* Now, let's look at what this area is like...

It is not fully unconscious, because sometimes there is *peripheral awareness of it*. You can't drive when you are asleep or totally unconscious, but you only need to give this activity your... well you guessed it... peripheral attention, and awareness.

The Conscious and the Subconscious Mind

However, *the subconscious is in contact with both the conscious and the unconscious.* Let's look at the last one first. In the *unconscious mind, we have all those mental processes that we are not aware of*. Automatic thoughts, dreams, forgotten memories etc. all "rest" in this part of our mind. When I say "part", I don't mean a "physical" place, because the mind is not the brain; the brain is physical, the mind is not.

The *conscious mind is where mental processes we are focusing on take place.* It is the center of our attention. If I am driving and talking to my friend, my conscious mind focuses on the conversation, not on driving. One of the reasons that we can do more than one thing at a time is that we can put our main focus on our main activity, and "peripheral awareness" on another one, usually a more automatic one.

The subconscious mind is out of our focal attention, but not fully unconscious. So, when Seb put the e-cigarette on the counter, he was focusing on buying a bun. On a "normal day" he would notice that he took out his e-cig (maybe by mistake), but this time he did not. So, he didn't shift his focus to the "unusual event", and he didn't notice it nor remember it at all.

We owe a lot to Sigmund Freud when it comes to the subconscious. Freud, as you may well know, is arguably by far the most famous person in the history of psychology, psychoanalysis, and psychotherapy. For Freud, things that are not needed immediately, but may or may not be needed at some stage soon, go into this area, where they are ready to be used, but "resting", like goods on shelves ready to be picked.

That indeed is what happens when you are driving, isn't it? If something happens, you immediately shift the focus from the chat you are having with your friend to your driving. And all the recent driving operations suddenly become very clear to you.

Conscious, Subconscious and Unconscious Mind

Although there is no exact calculation, experts tend to agree that *roughly 10% of the mind is conscious, 50 – 60% is subconscious and 30 – 40% is unconscious.* Not everybody agrees on this, but one thing seems to be met with consensus: *the conscious mind is only a small fraction of all our mind.*

A typical image we use to describe this structure of the mind is that of the iceberg. The conscious mind is the tip of the iceberg. The subconscious is the level floating up and down on the water surface, and the unconscious is that part that never reaches the surface of the sea.

How to Manipulate the Subconscious

Hold on, though, *how easy is it to make people do things subconsciously?* I am really sad and sorry to have to say that *it is fairly easy, easier than people may think, but it depends on many factors.*

A key technique to make people do things subconsciously is repetition. The first time you drive, you do it very consciously indeed. The more you do it, the less attention you pay to it, and the more subconscious it becomes. Oddly enough, doing things subconsciously may mean being very experienced and good at these things.

But, this, when it comes to fighting mind conditioning, also gives us a *key solution and principle to avoid, break and fend off mind manipulation: break the repetitiveness of the action.*

Let me give you a simple but fun (and useful) example. Do you always make the same typos? Like, many people spell "ten" instead of "the" or "ut" instead of "it" or they invert letters, like "teh" and "and" ... If they are repeated, it means that they are habitual, doesn't it? So, do you know how to correct these mistakes? **Turn the typos from subconscious to conscious!** If you type "teh" instead of "the", sit down and write "teh" wanting to write it, paying attention to it, and do it a lot of times... This way you will rewire your brain, and you will (promised) stop making that silly typo.

And if you do this, it will be your first, easy and practical rewiring and de-conditioning exercise! Well done!

How to Access the Subconscious

So, **how do things (thoughts, processes, desires etc.) get into the subconscious mind?** You have the answer now: **repetition of stimuli...** This is also true of small things, like the many small items we think we need every day. You see a new brand of candy one day, fine. You don't really care about it. But if you see it over and over again, then it becomes "familiar" and that convinces you subconsciously that it is "part of you" and that you "need it to be happy".

It gets a bit more sophisticated than that, and we will see it very soon. But **the core principle of** *advertising is repetition.* I don't know if you watch YouTube but it's a very good example of how they "invent our needs". If you do, you will notice that the ads on YouTube go in phases... At the time of writing, the "invest in the stock market phase" is over and the "take a marketing and managing course" is in full swing.

What's happening? Why so many ads of stock traders at the same time and then, as that is over, ads of webinars and online business courses? They really are the majority of all ads on that platform. More than 50% and at peak times far beyond that. Why?

Because *the more you see an ad about a product the more your subconscious is trained to recognize it as "normal" and if something is "normal and familiar" it is something you think you need.* Consciously you may well know you don't need that awful gadget. But as long as your subconscious is convinced, it just takes one "Seb moment" and you buy it!

Do you see how it works? Look back on your life and try to make a list of useless things you have bought... I'll see you back here in three minutes, just make a list, jot them down...

...

Here I am! I went out to water my roses; you should see how beautiful they are when they blossom... Anyway, it took me a second and I finished it. I bet you never managed to finish your list though, did you? Of course not!

This is proof that most of our minds are manipulated. But what matters most, this "shopping example" shows that *many if not most of our choices are manipulated.* You can consciously say that *all those useless gadgets were not the result of your conscious choice, and of your rational decision to buy them*. Some, maybe – and even those, well, if you found out that they were useless, then you had been conned anyway. And that is mind manipulation too.

Can I ask you another question? When did you buy most of those useless things? Think about it and I'll just check on my wisteria...

....

I'll tell you something about gardening and de-conditioning or rewiring the mind later in this book... For now, I'll just tease you... But it is to show you that the way out of mind manipulation can be very pleasant indeed. Where were we? When did you end up buying most of those useless trinkets? Maybe you said, "After I split up," or "When I was stressing about work," or maybe you focused on a long term, low level condition, like "When I am tired," or, frequently, "When I am down", or even "When I get back from work."

Fine, all these have one thing in common: *your conscious guard was down, and you were more vulnerable.* That's what possibly happened to Seb, though his case is a bit drastic, unusual. But the fact that when it comes to low level but pervasive mind conditioning, like advertising, when you are tired, stressed, ill (yes!), demoralized, worried etc. is when *your conscious mind has too much on its plate, and things that you would normally manage in the conscious mind end up being dealt with by the subconscious mind.*

And advertisers know this perfectly well. They know that when we are weak, they decide which behavior they can get from us. Which is, in this case, to buy their product.

Cultural Factors and the Manipulation of the Subconscious

Can this technique be used also for other ends apart from selling products? The concept of convincing someone that something is good or right subconsciously is the same as that of convincing the person that it is necessary.

In many cases, this can be traced to **cultural factors** too. If you are brought up in a family where every weekend, or worse every day, you do a certain thing, you will end up pushing this activity into the subconscious as "normal" and "part of yourself". And you will find it very hard to break away from it.

Let's take food for example. Fried fat is bad for you. Who does not know that? So why do so many people eat it all the time and in disproportionate amounts? There are two factors at play here:

- Continuous and ubiquitous advertising of "junk food".

- Having been brought up eating junk food.

If both happen together, then the mind manipulation and conditioning is very strong indeed! Let me explain...

You may say, "But junk food is very tasty." Yes... - and no! It is tasty because it has a very *recognizable* and *habitual* taste for those who like it. For example, I don't find it exceptional at all, I find it much less tasty than healthy food, honestly. But I grew up eating organic food from my father's garden and I *acquired a taste for it.* Even objectively, there are far more and more varied flavors in healthy food than junk food.

So, what is the difference? You see, most people are exposed to junk food commercials, especially in the USA. But not everybody falls for them, do they? People who were brought up eating healthy food are far less likely to feel they need junk food. What's happened then?

We can say that *junk food commercials target mainly people who have "internalized" the idea that junk food is very good, normal, part of their identity and "tasty".* And *"internalized" means received into the subconscious,* or, in very serious pathological cases, *even into the unconscious mind.*

And if your social and family background has done all the hard work of pushing ideas into your subconscious, then advertising will find it very easy to trigger the response they want from you.

And this is true also of other aspects of life, including views on life and political views. The process of *radicalization of terrorists and criminals is one of mind manipulation.* You will find it hard to turn an open-minded person who has had a very liberal childhood into a radical terrorist. But if you get someone who has already internalized wrong ideas, like discrimination, the idea that "some people are inferior" and even "subhuman", then it's easy to trigger a violent reaction, even on cue. Yes, it is!

Hitler knew this quite well, and that is why he insisted on the process of "internalizing" the concept of "superior and inferior races" and similar scientific and humanistic blasphemies... It does not matter even if you know it's not true; as long as you are brought up with that concept as "normal", there is an open door in your subconscious, a "button ready to be pressed", and when this is done, *you will do as ordered unless you have built a resistance to it.*

So, *understanding consciously that something is wrong or right is the first step towards building that resistance.* If you watch the Nuremberg trial, you realize that the Nazi leaders had totally internalized the idea that murdering millions of people was perfectly fine. For them, they were subhuman, because they had it in their subconscious, most likely in their unconscious and because their conscious did not confront them with the reality. Watching their straight faces when they say things like "I was very efficient with gas chambers," not even realizing what was wrong with it shows how far mind conditioning can go.

The First Step against Mind Manipulation

Let's take another example and look at this topic in even more detail, or better from another perspective. Do you know the first step towards beating an addiction? You need to admit (consciously) that you have one. Fine, it is only the first step and a small one. It's by no means enough... No way!

But it's the first step... However, some people have internalized the idea that they can't beat the habit. Let's take cigarettes as an example... Have you ever heard people say, "Yes, smoking is bad, but I can get run over by a car tomorrow, so why should I bother?" This and similar answers actually are not honest. I don't mean that they are not honest to you. In fact, they are! They are not honest to themselves. It is **their subconscious** that it **is telling them to invent excuses to deny or stop what their conscious mind is saying. They are, in other words, "self-deluded".**

Now, can you see how the conscious mind and the subconscious mind are continuously conversing? The same applies to the subconscious mind and the unconscious. The divide between conscious and subconscious is blurred and "shaded" if you wish... Let me explain...

Do you know when you go to sleep? If you are very tired, you just fall asleep immediately. Basically, you drop from conscious to unconscious in a matter of seconds. But if you are not so exhausted, there is a time in between... In that time, you are still thinking and maybe even imagining things, but it all appears random, doesn't it? It's like your mind is roaming free and you abandon logical and rational thinking...

That is technically called **hypnagogic phase**, and it is a time from when you stop being fully conscious and in control of your thoughts and when you actually "switch off" and fall asleep. This is a **window into the subconscious.** It does have thoughts, but they are not "guided", not "controlled", not "directed" ... The great Irish novelist James Joyce wrote a masterpiece chapter, the last one in *Ulysses* expressing Molly Bloom's hypnagogic phase. The longest chapter (40,000 words) with no commas, no full stops, just thoughts following each other freely.

We can imagine the subconscious as being a bit like that phase. But there is no "exact moment" when you switch in and out of it... It's more like "gliding into it" or "thoughts melting slowly" ... There isn't a clear-cut boundary. That "area of connection" between conscious and subconscious is where the **two parts of our mind talk between themselves.**

In fact, if you train yourself, when you are in the hypnagogic phase you can get out of it for a second, change your train of thoughts, then fall back into it. This is good to avoid negative thoughts; it will have a positive effect on your dreams...

But this also tells us one important thing that mind manipulators know quite well: *if the conscious mind keeps repeating an idea to the subconscious mind, the subconscious mind will accept it.*

When we are "fully awake" (fully conscious), *the conscious mind works like a "guardian" for information it filters through to the subconscious.* Basically, if I told you a whopping nonsensical lie now, like, "the Moon is made of cheese", your conscious mind would bounce it back as "false". But does this happen all the time? And is it possible to *"bypass the conscious mind"*?

Levels of Alertness in the Conscious Mind

One question at a time, as the first answer also explains part of the second. No, it does not happen all the time. *The more we are alert, the more we are capable of rejecting thoughts and information.* But let's go back to the hypnagogic phase to see this in action. In that time before you go to sleep, your thoughts are not divided into "good and bad", "real and false", "positive and negative" … You see, in the subconscious, thoughts and "things" simply "are". *We do not rationally discern between good and bad in our subconscious mind.*

You can already see how this is a goldmine for mind manipulators. If you pass a thought into the subconscious mind and then also pass the idea that that thought is good, you have literally bypassed the person's rational, moral, and ethical mind... **We decide between right and wrong in our conscious mind, not in our subconscious mind**.

Here is the big trick, isn't it? To start with, **we are not in "conscious mode all the time"**. If you catch someone when s/he is not in "conscious mode", you can easily pass on even wrong ideas, instructions, desires, etc.... This is because you don't have that "barrier", that "guardian" that "protection" you get when the conscious mind is switched on.

What's more, **even when we are conscious, there are different levels of alertness and of consciousness.** Let's stick to the word "alertness", which is far more correct, because Consciousness is a very complex topic, the "hard question" as scientists call it... Let's see this...

Think about yourself during the day, from 1 to 10, how alert would you say you are:

- Just after you wake up.
- After drinking heavy coffee.
- When you are working.
- When you are watching TV.
- After a heavy meal.

...

I was thinking about growing some herbs in my garden... What do you reckon? They keep pests away... Sorry, you know I take these breaks to do some gardening... Yes, you may have given different numbers, but for sure, you will have noticed that your alertness levels change throughout the day. For sure after heavy coffee, you are more alert. After waking up really depends on the person, as you know...

But the one I am most interested in is when you watch TV... The fact is. **When you watch TV your alertness levels drop significantly.** In fact in the long run, it makes you sleepy. What does this mean? That *the commercials you see on TV have a better chance of bypassing your conscious mind than others...*

But this is not only true of commercials: it is true of the news, information, ideas, opinions... The power of the television is far bigger than what people think...

Now, do you understand why so many experiments on mind control focused on subjects under the effects of psychotropic drugs? I would like you to think about it for a moment...

...

Whichever way you put it, let's see if you agree with what I am about to say: *experiments on mind control focus on people under the effect of psychotropic drugs because these induce altered states of consciousness. The researchers wanted to find out how changing your conscious state aided or prevented mind manipulation…*

It is not simply a matter of awareness, don't get me wrong. Consciousness is a vast topic. Actually, now Consciousness studies is becoming a whole new discipline, a branch of psychology but also of philosophy and anthropology (even physics actually!) But let's stick to the main concepts.

Your mind's alertness level can be changed artificially. In fact, the list of things that lower or your alertness is huge:

- Fatty foods
- Sugary drinks
- Dairy products
- Video games
- The television
- Social media
- Stuffy and polluted air
- Fluoride (this has a long-term effect on the mind).

These are actually "drugs" in the technical sense; they have a psychotropic effect on the mind. And note that most of what the modern world pushes for (in ads and not only) is within this list!

Activities and Substances that Raise Alertness

"Are there things that raise our level of alertness," you're rightfully asking? Yes, and we will see them all in detail, because these are the solution. Because not each single one is good... You see, as I said, it is slightly more complex than "simply being alert"; it's *"being alert in the right way" that matters.* But I am not going to keep you guessing for ages...

Here are some *practices and substances that make you alert in the right way:*

- Water
- Green tea
- Sleeping well
- Fresh air
- Contact with Nature
- Meditation
- Yoga
- Relaxation
- Martial arts
- Reading
- Vegetables
- Raw and unprocessed food

No, coffee and cocaine, even cigarettes, for example, make you very alert, but they only switch on part of your mind, and they leave the other part open to influence... Got the tick?

Bypassing the Conscious Mind

Now, on to the second question. As we said, you can now see how manipulation lowers your alertness levels and how we are not always 100% alert anyway... But now I am going to ask you a question.

I will ask you to stop reading for a minute and note down everything you can actually perceive, from the smallest noise to the quality of the air, smells, aromas, perceptions of light, voices, even far away in the background...

...

You won't believe how peaceful it is out in my garden... And you're seeing why I am linking gardening and preventing mind manipulation already... My little friendly hide and seek game is almost up... I'll come clean very soon.

I can tell you what I perceived though... I heard birds chirping, I smelt flowers (it's spring here where I am writing), especially daffodils, I felt a light breeze and, unfortunately, very much back in the distance, the noise of cars... There's a road about a mile from here, not a busy one, but I heard a car swish by...

You will have noticed different things, but for sure one thing we have in common. We could not perceive these things when we were intent on reading and writing... the same happens when you are talking, driving etc.... How many advertisements are there on the road? You actually see them, even if you are not aware of them... So, they bypass your conscious mind, and your judgement!

It is very easy to bypass the conscious mind with low level stimuli. These go under the radar of our alertness, because of course, we have a limited level of perception. We cannot focus on everything all the time, can we? And if you "receive them but you are not aware of them" they do not meet your conscious judgement, instead, they speak straight to your subconscious!

So, we have seen that *a key trick of mind manipulation is to bypass your conscious mind and speak straight to your subconscious mind*. This is done by:

- *Altering your level of awareness.*

- *Using low level but repeated stimuli that "go under the radar" of your conscious mind.*

Fortunately, there are solutions. For example, did you know that you can actually ***train your conscious mind to be far more alert?*** And because I am not so evil and I can't keep you waiting for solutions any longer, we are going to talk about it, right now!

Actually, I am going to do a spot of gardening first, but I'll be back as soon as you turn the page. Promise!

Chapter 3 – Training Your Conscious Mind

Welcome back! I bet you want to know about my "spot of gardening" now… Well, I just looked around my garden for things to do… It's quite nice, you see… that part of gardening where you just go round and let the garden tell you what it needs. It's nice in the morning. It's also a way of *training your mind to become aware of quiet stimuli…*

You see, it's so easy to focus on a noisy car passing by, or a person shouting in the streets, or a glaring commercial sign, or a massive flat screen… It's much harder, at least to us modern people, to let the odd sick leaf, maybe just discolored, catch your attention…

This is made worse by the fact that we live in a world where we are continuously bombarded with strong stimuli vying to catch our attention. And as you know, it's with the low level, hardly noticeable stimuli that they manipulate us. Even if we look at *grifters*, they *do the conjuror trick of distracting you with very showy and visible gestures with one hand and carrying out the trick with the other.* The concept is the same: *making sure they can bypass our attention.*

Increase Your Basic Attention and Awareness Levels

So, the very first solution would be to ***increase our basic attention and awareness levels!*** Everybody has his and her basic attention and awareness levels. They do change according to many factors, including:

- ***Stress***

- ***Mental fatigue***

- ***Physical fatigue***

- ***Illness***

- ***Personal situations***

- ***Worrying***

... and other factors.

These of course will lower your awareness levels. So, one thing to do is to **reduce these factors.** The simplest solution is to **have a healthy life.** But of course, this is not always possible, and I fully understand you. There are work problems; there are family problems; you may live in a chaotic city; there can be unforeseen events etc....

On top of that, *most of modern life is designed to keep us nervous, stressed, and constantly tired.* So, leaving the modern way of life would be an excellent – if drastic – solution. Among the least "mind controllable" people on the planet you will find monks... of any spiritual or religious persuasion. Why? To start with they are not under the constant stress of most people's lives. Secondly, they have actively trained their minds to be more aware. But...

What Does It Mean "to Be Aware"?

Being aware does not mean being edgy and nervous. There is this weird idea (that comes from the business world actually) that if you are "hyper" you are "aware and productive". Nothing could be further from the truth. Even socio-economic studies show that this myth of "hyper means productive" is just that. The most productive people don't run around like headless chickens... they are usually calm, older (yes!) and they have built stamina and techniques...

"Hyper" people in fact are easily manipulated. They have a *very narrow focus; all* their thoughts are centered on that focus. So, their awareness is actually very low when it comes to everything else... You see the point?

So, what does it mean? It means a few things and it has some characteristics.

Good awareness:

- **Has wide focus,** not just in one object, but on everything that surrounds you. In fact, the more aware you are, the farther your attention can go.

- **Is calm and peaceful;** people who are highly aware of their surroundings do not fret or stress about things easily. **Peace means having your mind free from thoughts; these thoughts actually distract your conscious mind from external stimuli.**

- **It's constant through time;** of course, it changes too, but slowly and to lesser extents than people who have peaks and sudden drops do (sugary drinks cause this, and when you have a "drop" your awareness collapses, as teachers know quite well!)

- **It uses all senses;** the ability to rely in many perceptive forms and many senses is very important to avoid mind manipulation.

- **A person who has high awareness also has an open attitude to others;** by "others" we also mean animals and trees and even ideas.

Yes, it's the opposite you see? You may think that you can **close up to shield yourself from stimuli – but this is a mistake!** It means using a lot of energy and the trick is to **be aware of the stimuli and quickly "deselect" negative ones.**

But how can you do it in practice?

Activities That Increase Your Conscious Awareness Levels

I bet you already guessed that there are activities that actually help you improve your awareness skills and raise your awareness levels. Maybe you already know I will be presenting gardening among these – and you are right; I will!

Let me give you an example though... Do you know that when you train for many sports, especially professionally, they teach you how to keep your eyes focused on the ball (for example) and at the same time look sideways to check what the other team members and your team members are doing? Well, *that* is actually awareness, not being totally focused on a page (paper or virtual) or on a specific client!

So, here we go, some activities that will increase your awareness... I am presenting them to you now, before everything else, for two reasons:

- **They are "groundwork"; they help your overall ability to counter mind manipulation.**

- **They take time – to learn, to be effective on your awareness and even to choose**...

So, start now!

Sports – Especially Team Sports

Sports teaches you a lot in terms of awareness, as we have seen. They teach you to be aware of the game, to focus on one point while keeping others within your peripheral vision. They teach you to keep an eye on your team and the competing team. They teach you to pick on small signals, from your team members and from your adversaries too.

You also have to heighten your attention during games (and training), and like with all things, practice makes perfect and training a skill or a sense actually improves it!

They also teach you stamina, a wonderful skill (or is it a quality?) that can really make a huge difference in life, not just when it comes to mind manipulation. They also have other great beneficial effects too. For example, when you are playing sports you are usually in a "free zone" from mind manipulation.

Finally, they reduce your stress levels overall and they make you healthier.

Strolling

Strolling is physical activity, but not actually a sport... Still, it has excellent qualities when it comes to improving your awareness skills. When was the last time you actually took a stroll? Just for the sake of it, I mean? Dashing to the corner store to buy salt is not strolling! Oddly enough this activity is far less common than we may imagine. Some people hardly ever take a stroll, and most do it once a week or so...

But strolling, ***especially in a natural place***, teaches you to allow your senses to be guided by the environment. You see we spend most of our lives ***directing senses towards stimuli***, and we lose focus on **what our senses pick up without us looking for it...** This second type of perception, ***passive perception*** (as opposed to ***active perception***) becomes "demoted" even fossilized in our minds...

And ***it's through passive perception that manipulation takes place.***

Strolling is also good for your health and stress levels. And it can also help you clear your mind.
So, if you really have no time to take up any other activity, promise that you will go for strolls every day. Yes, every day...

Martial Arts

Martial arts is literally designed to improve your awareness levels. They are just impressive. If a football player is aware of the teammate running next to him or her and of the adversary coming to intercept the ball, well... Compare it to a martial art master who knows if someone is simply looking at them – of course from behind!

Secret agents and special forces learn martial arts just for this reason; you become aware of all "presences", even those you cannot physically see. And you become aware even of the smallest stimulus, of a twig breaking in the forest, for example...

Naturally, martial arts teach stamina like few other sports, and in fact you can keep practicing them till you are very old, even till your death if you are healthy. But they are also good against stress and great for your health.

If you can, martial arts would be an ideal choice.

Meditation

Meditation is the best way to **clear your mind and relax**. You see, our minds are quite talkative in most cases. They keep talking to themselves all the time. Think about it, you hardly spend a minute (in most cases) without thinking rationally every day. What is more, the modern world encourages lots of verbal, rational thinking.

And **when we talk to ourselves with rational thoughts our awareness of external stimuli drops.** So, doing meditation is excellent against mind manipulation. It teaches you to "stop that voice at the back of your head" which, in most cases is distracting you from other things and stimuli.

It also teaches you to use all your senses; when you meditate, you perceive smells, sounds, colors, light, even gravity, heat, moisture, feelings, emotions, states of being... the list is longer than we think...

Finally, meditation actually increases mental ability and IQ (and EQ) levels, and many studies show it, and it does it very fast! According to neurologist

Fadel Zeidan and psychologist Paula Goolkasian, it *only takes four days (!!!) of meditation to see clear improvements in cognition* (mental abilities)! Their research appeared in the peer reviewed journal *Consciousness and Cognition* in June 2010 and it is titled 'Mindfulness and Meditation Improve Cognition: Evidence of brief mental training', if you want to know more.

Finally finally (sorry), it's excellent against stress and it builds inner peace.

Visiting Parks and Other Natural Places

Being in contact with Nature is an excellent cure for stress. It is no hippy hypothesis: the science is out and being in touch with Nature has healing properties. But apart from the direct effects it has on your physical wellbeing, as with all things healthy, it also positively affects your mental wellbeing.

Just the idea of cutting off the "hum of the city" for some time is excellent for your mind and awareness levels. But apart from the background hum, there are all those violent noises and visual stimuli which literally tire our brains. Especially in modern cities. An old town with pedestrian roads and old signs is not the same as a modern city with neon signs and a cacophony of clashing noises.

What is more, the modern world overwhelms our senses; sight, hearing and smell in particular. Taking a break from this and instead allowing our senses to re-align to gentle, natural stimuli is perfect to improve your awareness skills and level.

Of course, this activity too is good against stress. So… remember that outing to the nearby national park? Maybe it's time to get a picnic hamper?

Mindfulness

Mindfulness is a lesser-known practice unless you are into healing practices. But it's growing very fast and as you can see there is very strong academic evidence that it increases your mental and sensory abilities quickly and significantly.

Mindfulness is a very special "activity" because it is based on "letting your senses talk to you". You can see how this is *just perfect to train your senses and passive perception.* And mindfulness can be practiced anywhere and for any span of time. You can do it when you are queuing at the post office, while at work, while walking, while eating… As long as you suspend judgement and rational analysis and just "enjoy your senses" it works and it does not matter what you are doing and for how long.

Eating Slowly

While we are at it, slow down your eating... Even this can help you improve your senses and awareness levels – as well as your digestion... and it makes you slim down... but it gives you more energy and better nutrients!

We have lost our correct relationship with food... We tend to eat fast and "assault food"; this teaches us to focus on "strong stimuli and active perception". Eating slowly, on the other hand, teaches you to "listen to food" and taste is such an ancestral and visceral form of awareness... Then of course, eating involves sight, smell etc....

Painting and Other Arts

Take up painting, take your easel and go to a park...Sit there for hours and try to express what that wonderful landscape is telling you. It's not just a beautiful hobby (at least, and Art, anyway...) It is meditation on one level, it is expression on another level.

It teaches you to let "the world with all its stimuli and nuances" speak to you... And of course, it heightens your awareness and ability to recognize passive stimuli. It's also a good way to clear your mind and relax!

Gardening

We got here! You see, gardening is a bit like meditating, it is mindful, it is a nice hobby, it can even be productive, but there is more... It teaches you to be in touch with Nature, and it's a bit like martial arts: very harmonic. It too teaches you to recognize passive stimuli. It increases your awareness levels, and it widens your focus...

No need to say that it's also good physical activity, and is excellent against stress....

So, well, can I close this chapter with a "hippy" statement? *Mind manipulation uses the most appalling techniques and has carried out horribly cruel experiments, but the cure can be fun – in fact you can even avoid it and heal it with flowers!*

Chapter 4 – Signs and Symptoms of Mind Manipulation

How would you know if someone is trying to manipulate your mind? Are there clear signs and symptoms that someone is working on your subconscious mind to make you do what they want? You're in luck! The answer is actually a resounding yes!

But first of all, *remember to read signs together, not individually.* Imagine you go to your doctors with a complaint… For example, you feel tired and fatigued. That is the clear symptom that something is not 100% right with you. But is that enough for a good diagnosis? And, above all, would a good doctor not ask you more questions, look for other symptoms? Of course she would (or he would)! Your doctor may ask you a whole range of questions like how your appetite is, your sleep, if you have had lifestyle or dietary changes, if you are taking any medication etc.

So, let's take a leaf out of a professional doctor's book and do the same: *when you notice a sign or symptom of mind control, look for others before you draw a conclusion.* But why do I keep saying,

"Signs and symptoms"? Aren't they the same? In some cases, yes – in ours they are not.

The Difference between Signs and Symptoms of Mind Manipulation

For the sake of our topic, there is a clear and important difference between signs and symptoms of mind manipulation. It's because in mind manipulation we always have at least two participants: a manipulator and a victim.

So, we need to distinguish between what we find out by observing the manipulator and what we find out by observing the victim... I think you already know what I am going to say now...

- *By symptom, we mean a detectable effect of mind manipulation on the victim.* In extreme cases, these can be quite disturbing, like blank stares etc. But in most, less serious cases, they are much lighter symptoms. That is good, but it has a flip side: they are harder to detect.

- *By signs, we mean behaviors, words or actions we detect in the manipulator which indicate that s/he is trying to manipulate our mind.* You will notice typical use of words, patterns etc. which should raise suspicion… We'll get to them straight away.

Spotting Signs of Mind Manipulation

You will need to keep a close eye on the ***person and / or medium*** you think is manipulating you if you have some suspicions. Nowadays, very often the manipulator is "remote", hidden "behind a screen" or "behind a telephone". Do you get annoying cold calls trying to sell you something? I do… And I also know why they prefer a cold call to a face to face transaction… It's quicker, maybe, but there is also another reason: you cannot see the interlocutor so s/he can hide body language signs that s/he is lying to you.

Do you get lots of ads on social media? Well, be aware that behind every post or every pop-up window, there is ***a person (company) with a clear intention, and that intention is to get you to do something…*** Then it may be more or less honest, and even this is very much up to your standards… If you want my personal advice though, keep those standards very high! I do…

But which signs can you look for? There are some ***areas, patterns, and techniques that often give away the manipulator's intentions.*** And we are going to see them right now.

Repetition

You knew this was coming. We talked about it with the example of advertisements. But even if you are face to face with someone who is trying to sell you something, beware of repetitions! Listen to **salespeople** and you will find that they **repeat key selling points, key words, phrases etc.** That shows that they are very keen to get you to fall for these concepts.

I'll give you a funny example... Once I went to visit a flat, and it was so small I could not believe it! It must have been 200 sq feet maximum. There wasn't even room for a small cupboard... The estate agent, a very nice lady, of course was a bit at a loss, but I went a bit along with her, and she kept repeating, "It's convenient" ... The fridge was not "tiny" (and you couldn't even open it while you were in the kitchen you had to get out and open it!) It was "convenient". The fact that the inky storage space was in a hole with the electrical panel and the boiler was "convenient".

You get my point. She was in a bad selling position, but still she repeated the only selling point she had. Or thought she had at least! But this leads us straight into the next point, because the example is quite fitting too.

Doublespeak

If you have read *1984* by George Orwell, you will know quite well what that is. If you haven't read it, may I give you a little reading suggestion? It's a novel everybody should read. Ok, in *1984* there's a dictatorship that tries to control everybody's mind. And it does it in many ways, but one is *controlling the language and changing the meanings of words.* Using a word with the wrong meaning is called *doublespeak.*

It is very common indeed; newspapers use it all the time and promote it. Especially when it comes to politics and political views. Of course, the USA has seen massive use of doublespeak in recent years, but I will give you an example from outside...

Not long ago, in Italy, there were demonstrations, like normal demonstrations, nothing violent or anything. People marching peacefully in the streets. The newspapers started calling them "antagonists". Now everybody expressing an opinion is an antagonist to the opposing opinion, right? But "antagonist" sounds bad, as if you are "against the reader" not against injustice or even the loss of democracy (which is what they were demonstrating against) ...

That is a clear example of doublespeak. And newspapers and the media use it all the time and consistently. Doublespeak words just spread very fast and become established, by doing this, the **perception of reality people have is changed.** In Italy, they were clearly trying to present people who were actually demonstrating to uphold the Constitution as "the enemy" (and "antagonist" and "enemy" are very similar in meaning).

I must say this was one of the few cases where there was an outcry about the use of doublespeak and if the papers have not fully stopped using the word, they are using it far less now. This is something sociologists should study, because to my knowledge it's quite rare that doublespeak gets challenged, but it shows that if you do, it "pushes it back".

And that gives us a good clue on how to protect ourselves from mind manipulation. But we will talk about it in detail later.

Over-Emphatic Language

Now, US citizens are naturally (culturally?) emphatic when they talk. But within the cultural parameters of the people involved, using over-emphatic language is usually a sign of wishing to manipulate. Think about those old adverts you would see on TV. The key strategy was to emphasize how cheap the cars were, how "great quality" they were etc. Words were often over the top; things like "The best second hand cars in the country!"

Salespeople will often say things like, "This is a once in a lifetime chance," or, "The best on the market," etc. This excessive emphasis is an attempt to convince you, to change your mind, even using "exaggerations" or faking enthusiasm.

Now, there are really enthusiastic people, and maybe for good reason. People may really love an idea, an object, a person, a work of art etc.… But in most times, especially with salespeople, politicians, and the like, the speaker is not actually all that enthusiastic about it… Trust me; it's a show. And in many cases, we can spot it very easily.

The problem is that we have become accustomed to fake enthusiasm, so, this too often goes under the radar of our conscious observation… I have always found fake enthusiasm "grating and annoying". So, when a salesperson uses it, it actually works against his or her purpose and aim. If you can find it in yourself to feel the same distrust and rejection for fake enthusiasm, you will have a powerful tool to defend yourself from manipulation.

Empty Claims and Incorrect Use of Data

Fake emphasis and empty claims are related and often occur together. These two can be very good signs to tell you that someone is trying to manipulate your mind. What are empty claims? These are claims that have no evidence, but also claims where the evidence is picked on purpose. A typical manipulation technique is to **choose only those facts that are useful to the manipulator and ignore the others.**

Unless you know the topic you are talking about in detail, this is often difficult to understand. However, note a typical pattern here: the manipulator starts with some statistical data, which can also be true, but it is taken in isolation and only used to prove that his "pitch" is right. The manipulator will not stop on the details, context etc. of the data. He or she just uses it and jumps into the selling pitch straight away.

Have I talked to you about YouTube ads of online courses and webinars? They very often use this pattern. I'll simplify but the gist is this: "50% of businesses that fail don't use the right marketing technique. Our course will teach you just that."

To start with, do we actually know that the course teaches the right marketing technique? I mean, it looks like it because it gives us some data. But that's a mystification. Why? The data may well tell us the problem, but it says absolutely *nothing* about the validity of the course.

But the fact that they say it very fast and one following the other *makes it seem as if the data backs up the validity of the course or webinar.* It is not illegal, but it falls well under my bar of "correctness". To me it shows that they are ready to "bend the truth" to obtain something from you... Draw your own conclusion.

In my example (which I have slightly changed for copyright reasons), then, there's another "twisted fact. Note: "50% of businesses that fail don't use the correct marketing technique" only puts two details together, but does not link them. Put simply, we don't know if the lack of the correct marketing technique is t*he reason why they failed*... Maybe even 50% of those that don't fail use the wrong marketing technique?

Yet to the vast majority of people not even reading the data, but hearing it, delivered fast, maybe when you are half distracted, the ***impression is that the data backs up what the manipulator is saying and will say next; but it's just spin!***

Before parting with your hard-earned money, before making any important decision, ***beware of spin doctors and spun stories...*** Those ads, to be honest, struck me as being very much below my standards, very "insistent" even "aggressive".

Insistence and Aggressiveness

I would by any means avoid anyone who is insistent or even use "aggressive marketing techniques". These are clear signs that they want something from you, and they cannot get it by simply giving you the facts and asking you if you actually need it, want it, or even can afford it or not.

They are trying to:

- *Prevent you from thinking properly, and reflecting on what they are saying.*

- *Prevent you from weighing pros and cons.*

- *Prevent you from fully and clearly understanding what is being proposed.*

- *Give you a fake sense of necessity, urgency etc.*

I am here talking about the greengrocer at the market who shouts out, "Ripe tomatoes 50% off! Hurry up!" That is straightforward, you see, he or she is possibly telling the truth and not hiding the fact that s/he wants you to hurry up...

When they actually hide the fact that they are hurrying you up, however, then it's a problem...

Linking Unrelated Things, Images, Thoughts

Think vodka, gin etc.… I know, you already got a picture of "summer holiday" and "half naked women" (or men) and "party time on the beach" in your mind. Why? You know why… For years they linked the idea of spirits with these images in commercials.

They are totally unrelated… Would you really naturally go for vodka when it's 100 degrees in the shade? Maybe a cold soft drink, maybe a beer, an ice pop? Vodka, really? And before these ads, people thought of bearded men dressed in heavy furs in the snow when they heard the word "vodka". Gin too was linked to "poor and destitute people in northern Europe", not a catchy, "sellable" image…

But like you saw in *Clockwise Orange,* and now you know how Behaviorism works, you will understand that linking half naked women on a beach with vodka is like giving food to dogs when you ring a bell… The dog will salivate even when the food is no longer there – and I'll stop the sentence here… But that's exactly how they are treating you…

Body Language

Body language is a whole branch on its own, and if you want to know more, I will add a link in the resource page to study body language and how to use it against mind manipulation. For now, be aware that *incoherent, contradictory, and nervous body language may be a sign of dishonesty, thus an attempt to manipulate you.*

Of these, nerves can easily be due to other reasons, and you always need to read all signs in conjunction. Look out for signs like:

- *Hiding hands.*

- *Avoiding eye contact.*

- *Keeping physical distance.*

- *Closing up (crossing legs, arms etc.)*

- *Sneering.*

- *Trying to gain a "vantage point, a higher position".*

- *Contradictory signs in general.*

Body language is one of the best ways of telling if a person is "comfortable" or "uncomfortable" with what s/he is saying, and even great liars are never fully comfortable with lies...

Talking too Fast

We have already seen this, but it's worth stopping on it for a second. Yes, expert manipulators will use a speed which is adapted to the victim: just a bit faster than the victim can manage. And by manage, we don't mean hear, but "understand fully".

In other cases, like when you see posts in your timeline, then they are timed so that the average person will never be able to comprehend them fully unless they expand the post and read it…

Some ads are fast, on purpose. They want to sound intelligent; they also want to look like they have a lot to say; it creates a false sense of urgency and, of course… they bank on viewers not understanding what they are saying fully, correctly, or critically.

Elusiveness

And of course, you can get as much from what people don't say as from what they say, and how they say it – maybe even more! We will look at techniques for how to reflect on what people say later on. But for now, keep these three ideas in mind.

- *Hang on to what you think the person has not said, and you noticed during the speech.* Make a mental note when you feel there's something missing. You can do it in many ways. Of course, you can write it down, if you have a chance. You can make a mental note if you have a good memory. I count, using my fingers... I count a finger at every question I have, every doubt I have, and keep them in mind. And you know what? It seems to put manipulators on the back foot. They will notice you, and they will know their story is not working...

- *After the encounter, the speech, the advertisement, the meeting etc. take time to reflect on it and ask questions about it.* This is even more essential if it is an important matter. Never buy anything of value on the spot, take your time... The same applies to big choices in life. You have a *right to reflect and consider all the points, doubts etc.* And if there are points that are not clear, if you have doubts, again, make a note. Write them down... *The more important the choice is, the closer you need to be to 100% certainty.*

But let me tell you a trick... You can turn the "missing information" to your advantage. How? Here is the third idea to keep in mind:

- **If you have doubts, or feel something is missing, ask questions.** To start with, you should never trust anyone who does not even want to be questioned. But sometimes we can become a bit "shy" just when we should not be...

  By all means, ask questions about what does not convince you, and keep pressing. Even if there is nothing specific you have doubts about, always ask questions about details. Then, keep an eye (ear) on what the response is like: is it confident, straightforward and exhaustive? Is the other person trying to evade the point? Or the answer is not as straightforward as you would like?

Whether the person's words are elicited or not, the **elusiveness in a speaker is always a very good sign that s/he is hiding something from you.**

There is, of course, the chance that the person simply does not know the answer. This, again, is something many people can "sniff out". Ignorance in itself is not "incriminating", but if you notice a willingness not to answer, and a few other signs that go with it, then you are really on to something.

Symptoms of Mind Manipulation

Let's now turn to the victim. The symptoms of mind manipulation are many, varied and they depend a lot on the gravity of the manipulation.

A good example would be Othello, the protagonist of the eponymous tragedy by Shakespeare, and a play I would suggest you watch or read if you are interested in mind manipulation. At first, he is fine, he only becomes a bit suspicious when Iago "sows the seed of jealousy" in him. Then, he becomes nervous, more suspicious, he "wants more and more information about his wife Desdemona"; he then becomes antisocial, he becomes distracted from his work, he becomes paranoid and, in the end, even murderous.

This is a play, but it shows the **escalation of symptoms as the mind manipulation progresses.**

At the same time, when you are under continuous and low-level **mind manipulation, you most likely will have no symptoms at all.** The trained eye may notice them, but for most people, some symptoms are seen as "normal behavior".

Now, let me give you a simple example. I have a friend; his name is Jeremy and he's overweight. He knows he is, but despite all this, Jeremy cannot go by a fast-food restaurant without stopping at least, casting the desirous eye to the window, and in many cases, he walks in...

Even if he did not walk in, you would still, from an external, objective, and independent perspective, notice that there are symptoms of mind control, in this case...

Cravings and Unhealthy Interest in Something

Cravings for food, alcohol, shopping items, cigarettes etc. are all clear symptoms of mind manipulation. "Hold on," you may say, "cigarettes are addictive." True, but they are part of the mind manipulation strategy themselves, while also being the aim of the manipulation. It happens a lot with addictive products (and remember that sugar, fat, coffee etc. are all addictive substances).

Also, morbid interest in a topic or "fetish" (by no means sexual fetishes, others, like the new phone, a brand, an item of clothing, a particular car etc.) can be clear symptoms of mind manipulation. I think the explanation here is straightforward. It's fine if you like something in a healthy way; but think about cell phones, in some cases, the interest in the new model is literally morbid. Long queues to get model 1235782901457/bis-ABRTF75 of the famous "uPhone" (I didn't want to give them a free commercial!), especially with people who already have model 1235782901457/bis-ABRTF74 is not healthy behavior.

These people actually think they are "cool", because they appear as the "top of society" especially in particular parts of society, modern, technological, urban, "connected" etc.... The reality is different; in some respect, they are more serious than Jeremy. His addiction is really bad, don't get me wrong; but at least he knows he has it and he does not feel "cool" anymore for eating fast food.

Note how all this can be explained away with the old bell and salivating dog... They want the new phone not because they actually need it, but because they associate it with *social clout (a very common "reward" in mind manipulation).*

These are the most common *low-level manipulation symptoms.* At higher levels, the list is quite frightening, but we will go through it fairly fast, because they are comparatively (sigh!) rare, and in these cases, the victims would need professional help.

Symptoms of Serious and Advanced Mind Manipulation

You know by now that mind manipulation can reach unthinkable levels. Usually, low-level mind manipulation has few visible symptoms. But when it becomes serious, then there can be a long series of symptoms, including:

- *Eating disorders*; here we are not talking about Jeremy's case (which could still be an eating disorder), but people who are being manipulated for things other than food, and yet the manipulation affects their eating habits.

- *Sleeping disorders*; these are quite common, sometimes even at low levels, with dreams about a product, waking up wanting to smoke etc.... But in serious cases we talk about either insomnia, uneven and discontinuous sleeping patterns, or also unusual dreams or even continuous nightmares. The latter is tantamount to torture, and many targeted individuals report appalling things, like, "Every dream for months was a nightmare" ... These are extreme cases (and many got compensation for this).

- *Problems socializing;* it is not unusual that people under severe mind control find it hard to relate to others; in many cases, their plea for help is in itself a problem. People do not understand what they are going through and they themselves are often unaware of the root problem and they cannot explain it, nor prove it, very often. So, acquaintances, friends, and even family may think they are "weird" or even "crazy"...

In other cases, anyway, the strain mind manipulation puts on victims can result in lowered social skills, the need to sleep, to stay alone, to avoid crowded places etc. This and other behavioral patterns can negatively impact on their social life.

- *Addiction;* severe mind manipulation can be a real strain on the individual, as we said. Quite a few turn to alcohol or other drugs, including prescription drugs... If you met them and listened to their stories as I did, you couldn't possibly blame them for it.

- *Inefficiency at work;* yet another consequence can be that people lose focus at work, which can also happen in small doses at low level mind manipulation. The time you spend browsing for the new iPhone model is not really spent efficiently for work. But in serious cases it can turn into a regular and unmanageable lack of focus. No need to say many targeted individuals lose their jobs, or find it hard to find another.

- **Mental blocks and "blanks";** strained minds sometimes stop when they are pushed. Also, serious mind manipulation interferes with the normal cortex workings of the brain. Some mental paths may be "cut" (weakened), or the brain and mind may become very tired, and the "lapse" or *lapsus* becomes common, at times frequent.

- **Memory loss;** this is common with everybody under strain, thus, it does happen that people under mind control end up suffering from memory loss.

- **Erratic behavior;** of course, mind manipulation has the aim of changing your behavior; this can have all sorts of side effects, including behavior that onlookers cannot explain logically. In serious cases, people may shout at "invisible things or listeners" in the streets, for example.

- **Repeating the same story;** some people who have suffered seriously from mind manipulation may keep repeating the same story, often about themselves, often about an injustice received, to people they meet, even very early on in the encounter.

- **Blank stares;** once you are "under" in serious ways, your eyes will look very intense at one stage, but looking blankly and past people. This is a sign of actual mind control. These are looks you find in people who belong to death cults, sects (and other cases, like secret service "unwilling agents" etc.)

- **Violent behavior;** this is a rare, extreme, and very serious symptom. It may happen because the person needs to release tension, in which case it is still bad, but not as bad as when the violent behavior is actually the aim of the mind conditioning operation. Yes, it is possible to get people to commit violent crimes through mind manipulation, the word "assassin" itself is a case in point.

And we shall close this chapter with an intriguing story, one you can add to the history of mind manipulation, one that shows how old it is and how efficient it already was almost a thousand years ago already, and one that tells you the origin of a word...

What is the origin of the word "assassin"? Assassins were actually a group of heretical Muslims of the Eleventh Century BCE. They lived in the Middle East, especially in Persia and Syria, and their actual name was *Nizari Ismailis.* Why then this "nickname?"

Well, they used to take a lot of hashish before going on murdering expeditions. I know, weed smokers nowadays are peace loving dreamers, mainly, but the fact is that when they smoked, they were told all sorts of stories about how fighting for their cause would send them to Heaven...

So, it was a way of manipulating their mind, like Pavlov did with dogs, or better almost like the CIA did with LSD and the Nazis with mescaline... The difference is that they were only manipulated with **positive reinforcements to stimuli**, not negative ones, so... Not so cruel (and effective) as modern mind manipulation...

Still, in Arabic, *"hasisi"*, *"al-Hasishiyyun"* or *"hashashin"* all mean "hashish eaters" and that was their nickname. It was then transformed into the Latin *"assassinunus"* and you can see that it is basically the modern English word we use nowadays: "assassin".

Imagine what they can do nowadays!...

But did I drop a little clue to what we are going to see next? Yes, I did! Because in the next chapter we are going to look at the very, very core of behaviorism in detail. You know a lot already, but this is going to give you a very technical insight and – of course, ideas on how to counter mind manipulation...

But can I ask you one thing before we move on? Would you do something you really like before you turn the page? Guess what? I'm going to look at my garden – you do what you like best, even for a minute...

Chapter 5 – Behaviorism, Positive and Negative Reinforcement

Did you fully enjoy what you did? No, don't tell me... I am not a curious person... Anyway, you are right – I couldn't possibly hear you... I haven't got mind reading skills, though apparently some people do, so we find out in the CIA files from *Project Stargate* reveal... The declassified files (2017) showed that they used mind readers to spy on the Russians from 1972 to 1995, a "hell of a cheap system," according to US Congressman Charlie Rose of North Carolina, of the House Select Committee on Intelligence...

This just shows you how far this side of "underground psychology" has developed... But you are safe with me and now I am going to tell you why I asked you to do something nice before reading this chapter... Because *I wanted you to associate reading this book with something positive...*

The difference with mind manipulators is that *I didn't force the reinforcement on you (a)* and above all *I came clean and was honest and open about using it (b).* That makes a huge difference from when you watch the proverbial vodka commercials with half naked women (and/or men) dancing on the beach... That's not something you choose and they (badly, ok…) conceal **making a link, a connection in your mind between a stimulus and a reinforcement.**

What is more, this **reinforcement can be positive or negative.** What we saw "between the chapters" was **positive reinforcement,** which, in Pavlov's case, was food for the dogs, for potential (male) vodka drinkers, it is the image (hope, desire etc.) of a beach party with half naked women (the odd half naked man thrown in makes sure that it is not only "targeted" at heterosexual males…)

Now, sorry, the word "targeting" that market experts use all the time always brings up a very bad feeling… Where were we then? There is a **reward, or positive reinforcement** but there can also be a **punishment, or negative reinforcement.** We will come to this last one in a minute…

Positive Reinforcement

Positive reinforcement is not in itself unethical, dangerous, "bad". In fact, while mind manipulators have developed ways of using it to "bend your will", it can be applied to very positive ends…

Think about the teachers you liked most at school; most likely they were those who noticed when you did or said something right, those who encouraged you, those who said little words like, "well done," or "great idea," or "good point!" They were, in short, those who used positive reinforcement.

Virtually all *modern pedagogues believe that good education is based on positive reinforcements.* Teachers now know that if they give rewards to students, they will encourage them, boost their motivation, their stamina, and even their willpower. Not only, but they also know that their students will love their subject, and pursue it (unless something negative happens), even after they are no longer students...

And I am asking you to go down memory lane now, and think about the subjects you liked, the ones you pursued after school, formally or informally... Now, think back to when you were a student: how did you feel about them? How did the teachers make you feel about these subjects? Take a few secs (as long as you wish, actually) to think about this and bring back some memories...

...

I didn't go to the garden; I actually did the same exercise as you did this time... All sorts of things come up when we go back to our school days... We remember the oddities of teachers, their weird behavior (we do, and better than their lessons!) But we also remember "good teachers and bad teachers" …

Sometimes we cannot put our finger on it, but with the good teachers we usually felt "safe", "understood", "encouraged" … in a word, "rewarded". Maybe you don't remember exactly, or maybe now you know about it, your memories will bring up those nice words, the smiles, the nods that the "good teachers" regularly used.

There are loads of studies that show that positive reinforcement can improve a student's academic success. This also works with parents and their children actually. And there are many studies that show that **positive reinforcement can improve behavior in children and pupils,** one such research papers is 'From Positive Reinforcement to Positive Behaviors: An Everyday Guide for the Practitioner' by Ellen A. Sigler and Shirley Aamidor, which appeared in *Early Childhood Education Journal,* Vol. 32, No. 4, February 2005.

This study confirms that positive reinforcement works, but unlike other studies it can also see the drawbacks: there's a funny passage in it, a hyperbole, an exaggeration, but maybe not even such a big exaggeration:

> *"It is true that when a child is engaged in a creative activity, like drawing or painting, if*

> *you indicate, "I like the color you are using,"*
> *you will indeed get an entire page of purple."*

I am sure you understand what the researchers are saying... But apart from the funny side, it has two important points in it:

- **Positive reinforcement is very powerful, and it can change behavior.**

- **Positive reinforcement must be used correctly and ethically.**

And this second point is exactly what we are going to see next.

Using Positive Reinforcement Correctly and Ethically

Would you think that the now famous vodka commercials use positive reinforcement correctly? Ethically? Do you think it is acceptable to encourage people to drink spirits, which cause all sorts of health and social problems by falsely associating them with partying on a beach with half naked people? Think about it...

...

These ads are fully legal, but I can hardly find what **good they want.** Unless we accept that "making money is always good", I have an ethical problem with these commercials. And I bet you had already suspected I did! Using what is proven to have an effect on people's psychology and behavior to cause self-harming behavior cannot be defined as good, nor as neutral, but only bad. They are therefore totally unethical.

Now, in the study by Sigler and Aamidor we cited before there is a clue: **you must make sure that the behavior you want to obtain by using positive reinforcement is positive, good...** And this means for the person you are encouraging too.

Developing stamina, confidence, willingness, and even interest in pupils and children is certainly good. Helping people break a smoking (drinking or drug) addiction is good too. You know they will benefit from using positive reinforcement.

But many advertisements show that **it is possible (but unethical) to use positive reinforcement to encourage negative behavior.** You can give a sweet (or tell him/her something positive) to a child every time s/he does something bad, like throw a tantrum, or worse... This way you will encourage the child to do it again.

This is why it is true that when a child throws a tantrum, you should not give him/her what they want. That teaches him/her that bad behavior has positive consequences.

Similarly, *breaking mind manipulation only uses positive reinforcement.* To stop, get out of, recover from mind manipulation, we can only use positive reinforcement. This may look like a disadvantage. I don't think so. I actually think it's a bonus... It means that getting out of mind manipulation is a positive experience.

Now, I'll ask you to do an experiment. Choose something you know you don't need but you want "too much". Something bad for you. Choose something fairly small at this stage. You know exactly where I am going: choose something you suspect you only crave through low-level mind manipulation.

It may be a product, unhealthy food often advertised on TV etc. It may be using social media... Don't worry; I am not asking you to give it all up completely. But take about a week. Once a day, when you want it, just renounce. But that's not the end of it... Replace it with something healthy (physically, mentally etc.) and pleasurable.

Instead of going on HeadBook (I like changing names of brands, just out of spite) or Trotter, listen to some of your favorite (uplifting, please!) songs.

Instead of the burger, cook (or get) something healthy but tasty, high quality... There's a lot to choose from nowadays. Instead of the sugary fizzy drink, get some freshly squeezed fruit juice...

Do it once a week... We will come back to this exercise later in the book, for now, just choose what you will do.

...

Done? Best of luck with this experiment. You already see that we will be using positive reinforcement to break a habit. For the time being, I simply want you to **build the idea and experience that life can be more pleasurable without that habit, that addiction.**

If you want to reinforce this even further, add two things to the experiment:

- *Write down how good you feel when you do "the other thing".*

- *Remember the pleasure you got from "the other thing" just before going to sleep.*

One will make a more memorable mark in your rational mind, the other will help your subconscious mind accept the new activity as "part of you and good". Both will fix the new "other activity" more firmly in your memory as positive.

But now on to the other side...

Negative Reinforcement

Welcome to the "dark side". And dark it is indeed. We have seen that while the original "assassins" were motivated to kill with lots of hashish and lies about a reward, the Nazis and the CIA even used torture to change people's behavior.

We need to step back a little in time though now. Just after the Second World War, a study that came out in 1948, by a US psychologist by the name of **B.F. Skinner**. He is famous for what is known as "the Skinner box". I could call it a "torture chamber for mice" but let me know if you disagree...

It is a cage, with an electrified grid as the floor, a green light and a red light, a loudspeaker, a lever that opens or not a food dispenser. You can see how it works; the loudspeaker gives a signal that tells the mouse that there may or may not be food. The mouse has to look at the lights: green means there is food (reward) and red means the poor little creature will get a "complimentary electric shock on the house". The mouse can either get the reward or the electric shock when it pulls the lever, according to the light.

Then guess what? The mouse quickly learns that when the light is red, that lever is better left untouched.

Skinner found out *three types of reinforcements:*

- *Positive*

- *Neutral*

- *Negative*

We have seen the first: the neutral has no effects, the third has strong effects. What's more - is that *negative reinforcement has very fast effects; fear acts very quickly on the victim's mind.* It does, in fact, work faster than positive reinforcement. The reason is actually simple: *when we are worried for our safety, it becomes a priority, and we want a fast solution.*

It also means that often we suspend critical thinking when we are scared and/or facing a threat to our wellbeing, happiness, even social status, or in extreme cases, safety and life.

Negative reinforcement is a very powerful tool.
Some people will say that it's more powerful than
positive reinforcement. It may depend on how
heavy the punishment is, but what matters to us is
not so much which is generically "stronger". What
we need to state is that ***negative reinforcement is:***

- ***Faster acting***

- ***Always unethical***

I mean, you can get permission to use very limited
negative reinforcement from a volunteer to an
experiment. That consent needs to be, however,
signed in full consciousness, compensated
(financially) and the extent of the negative
reinforcement must be very limited and never leave
any permanent or long-term consequence.

I can give you a bitter coffee, or if I want to overdo
it, a salty coffee for an experiment after you have
signed a full agreement and I have paid you for it…
This is in the name of science. That's about it… No,
an electric shock is not ethical. With or without
agreement and with or without even massive
compensation. It's not just illegal; it is a crime
against Humanity.

And now I will show you some of the horrible things
that have happened "on the dark side".

Uses of Negative Reinforcement

Unfortunately, people (even well-educated people) often forget the ethical issue and they like to cut corners and get quick results. So, guess what? Negative reinforcement has been used to change people's behavior even in institutional and "scientific" situations.

You will know that till not long-ago caning students (or other forms of corporal punishment) was acceptable. No, sorry, I got it wrong. It wasn't just acceptable. Educationalists swore by it. And of course, you would avoid making mistakes if you didn't want your knuckles birched, but you also became very wary about exploring (and presenting) new ideas. In the end, is education just "avoiding mistakes"?

Electro-shocks (or ECT, Electroconvulsive Therapy) have been used by so-called psychotherapists for decades, and in many countries the "therapy" is still not illegal, even if it's almost never used, and used with low electrical discharges. Well, it is torture, and torture is a crime against Humanity (we have seen a few already on the dark side...)

We have seen appalling experiments (even on children) with negative reinforcement and mind conditioning. The use of psychotropic and hallucinatory drugs like LSD was meant to worsen the effect of the punishment, to extreme levels (nightmarish, literally, just imagine being in pain and in a horrible nightmare sometimes for weeks on end...) Just thinking about it is sickening.

Lesser and more acceptable uses of negative reinforcement may be the "garlic nail polish" to make children stop biting their nails. But even that one raises all sorts of questions from a psychological point of view, for example:

- If a child bites his or her nails, this is usually a symptom of something deeper (insecurity, worry etc.) stopping the symptom does not solve the problem.

- Even worse, the child now can associate the attempt to relieve himself/herself from the problem with a bad experience.

- Then garlic is actually a super healthy food; are we sure we want our children to hate it?

On the whole we can safely say that very little good will ever come from negative reinforcement. And having said this, we will get out of the "dark side".

Hey, but don't jump with joy yet... We are going "somewhere in between" now.

The Trap: Positive and Negative Reinforcements Together

The effect of mind manipulation is heightened if you use both lights in Skinner's box, metaphorically speaking: *if you use both negative reinforcements and positive reinforcements you will have a huge effect on the victim.*

Guess what? Mind manipulators are very much aware of this. In serious cases, like with MKUltra and similar horrendous projects, these two forces were sometimes applied intentionally.

If you show someone that when s/he does something the punishment stops and not only, a reward starts, it's quite easy to condition this person to doing it as a habit. I will give you an example. Heroin, the drug… You see, people who use it feel bad when they are not using it, and very good when they use it. It becomes "second nature" to take it then. This is why the habit is hard to break.

If you give an electric shock to someone when this person for example waves with the left hand, and a reward when s/he waves with the right hand, you will soon find that the person not only will stop waving with the left hand, but will be very willing to wave with the right hand.

This concept works at all levels (of stimulus, reward, and punishment) and on all sorts of behavior. It can be drastic like the electric shock I mentioned, even more drastic if under the effect of psychotropic substances, or very light, like a simple smile and sneer... But maybe repeated over time and often.

Now, I will ask you a question... Do you use any social media? Have you ever posted something that got many "likes, stars, hearts, thumbs up, or positive comments"? Ok, we all did. But have you ever posted anything that got negative comments, people arguing with you etc.? If you have you know what it feels like.

Now, can you see that *social media has a system of rewards which is inbuilt, but a "hidden" system of punishments as well.* People who design these massive platforms know exactly what they are doing. They try them out in Beta format for a long time. They study users' reactions. And they know the social context they are working within very well...

So, what is the effect of likes for some posts and (sometimes long and exhausting) arguments for other posts? Which posts get the most likes? Which gets the most arguments? Think about it for a minute...

...

I hope you remembered to do something positive in the meantime. Maybe replaced a bad habit with a good and pleasurable one like we said at the end of the last chapter? Anyway, I am sure this exercise opened up a lot of pathways of investigation to you...

We will get round to discussing social media in great detail very soon. But for sure you will have noticed that **the posts that get most likes follow a trend, a pattern**. This trend depends on the "bubble" you are in and on very typical "online conversation modes". Memes get lots of likes. But memes also teach you to disrespect others.

How about the posts that get contradicted etc.? These are often critical posts, posts that don't form with what most people think, especially in your bubble. So, we can say that **the overall effect of rewards and punishments in social media is to make you conform to some social patterns and avoid critical thinking.**

And this is not little in terms of mind manipulation... But there is more, and a final point I would like to make: the **effect of society as negative reinforcement**

Social Negative Reinforcement

Did you notice that while the social media themselves don't have an inbuilt punishment system in most cases, they use the behavior of users for it? YoTube (it's the young version of the other "tube") does have thumbs down, but most other social media avoid them.

Still, if you say something that goes against what people who watch, think, or like, and especially if it goes against what a particular group of people dislike, people who like to "argue their case on social media"... well, if you have had a long argument on one of these, especially "Trotter", you will remember that you had a horrible time, even a whole horrific day.

Let's go back to our vodka commercials... Can you see any "implicit" and "covert" negative reinforcement given by social values and society in them?

...

I bet you did! The idea behind it is that you have to be "cool". Those ads are mainly positive reinforcement, but even there, you will find the little thought at the back of your mind that says, "These are the cool guys," and thus the sentence, for the vast majority of people, those who have felt "uncool" at school has a very loaded meaning. It means, "Hey, if you don't drink our vodka, you are not cool". And that is how many **commercials and other forms of mind manipulation use society, social "values" (beliefs), patterns, and traditions as negative implicit reinforcement.**

Now you can see how deep this system of negative and positive reinforcement is; it uses society, it goes deep into our subconscious and it can be very insistent, repetitive and all pervasive.

But we have a few ideas about how to get out of it now... It has to do with positive reinforcement, but also with replacing a bad, induced habit with a good, chosen one... And this is what we are going to see next. But take a break now and guess what? Do something nice, healthy, and pleasurable first!

Chapter 6 – Replacement Therapy for Mind Manipulation

Mind manipulation causes a form of addiction, as you now know. And what is the best way out of addiction? There are a few working strategies, to be honest, including changing life or lifestyle. But, honestly, not everybody can afford to get the first coach and leave everything behind for a new life... So, the most practical, the most adaptable, and often the cheapest way out is *replacement therapy.*

Do you know that I gave up smoking a few years ago? I had tried in many ways... I tried chewing gums, patches, pills... It never really worked till vaping came along... Vaping is simply strong, effective, and even a fashionable replacement therapy. And it works so well looking at the numbers that the tobacco Industry is really worried.

But do you know what my father told me when he saw me vaping? He said, "Son, I gave up from one day to the next – just with my willpower." Ok, some people may have done that in their life, but to start with, he "lied"; even my father, who does have amazing willpower, used candy sweets to get out of smoking... It's just a less effective replacement therapy, in the end.

Of course your life situation, commitments, quality, social relationships etc. are all factors that can help you succeed or not... And life has become more hectic and stressful. This means that it's harder on the whole to give up on bad habits and break addiction and mind manipulation...

In fact, communities and clinics for alcoholics and drug addicts are not in Manhattan and even fewer in Queens... They are in peaceful places, often in the countryside. They also offer that life change element that really works. For serious victims of mind manipulation, like targeted individuals, the suggestion of moving to a quiet place in the countryside is a very good one indeed. And these people have suffered so much that I do know some who have actually left their job and everything and moved to a peaceful place in the middle of nowhere...

For lesser problems, maybe selling your home is a bit too much to ask! So, let's stick to replacement therapy for the time being...

What Is Replacement Therapy

Most of us know roughly what "replacement therapy" means. It means *replacing a habit, substance, or behavior with another one you have chosen and which is healthier and better for you.*

But in the examples we have seen, we already have two types of replacement therapy. I said that my father changed smoking for eating sweets; I changed from smoking to vaping. For heroin addicts, the swap is from heroin to methadone in many cases... These are not the same "types" of replacements, are they? In fact, they are:

- ***Replacing the way a substance is used with another way (smoking – vaping).***

- ***Replacing a noxious substance (habit) with a less noxious one (smoking – candy sweets).***

These are typical replacement therapies. Note one thing, with vaping you can then easily reduce the amount of nicotine by degrees and reach no nicotine at all. The "smoking nicotine to vaping nicotine" is only the first step. The second step is the elimination of nicotine altogether. Store owners and assistants of vaping outlets actively encourage customers to reduce the nicotine till you get to naught in my experience, doing an excellent service to society.

The same idea applies to methadone and my father's candy sweets (and other food, mind you... most people who stop smoking eat more...) However, methadone has not proved that effective in the reduction phase...Anyway, the idea is that this replacement needs to go one way:

- *... all these replacements are then meant to reduce the quantity of the substitute substance/habit till you get completely out of the addiction.*

But when we talk about mind manipulation, we also need to look at a third type of replacement therapy... ready?

Mind Manipulation & Replacement Therapy

You have already started replacement therapy, have you not noticed? I asked you to change a habit by *replacing only part of the habit but with something totally different.* You see how this uses the same principle as "total replacement" therapy but instead of changing the whole substance/habit etc. with a "less bad one" all at once, and then reduce the less bad one... Here we ask you to introduce a positively good one, but start replacing the bad one by stages, till the positively good one has totally replaced that bad one.

We can use both strategies in mind manipulation cases; the latter though is particularly useful with mental patterns and rewiring... *Mind conditioning often leads you to thoughts you do not actually*

want. It is at this stage that we can rewire the brain and strengthen positive thought patterns instead.

We will see this better when we talk about rewiring the brain, but ***the more you follow a thought path the stronger it becomes.*** The more you think, "I like sweets," the more it will be easy to think about it, the more often this thought will come and the more you will actually believe that you like them.

How about if, just at the "juncture" in your brain where the street "I like sweets" starts with you getting a fork, and then you get "I love fruit a lot" instead? At first, this second thought path will be small, like a little animal trail in the forest. But the more you repeat it, and you give it a strong, pleasurable positive reinforcement, the more this path will widen and become clear... Till it's bigger and more pleasant than the "I love sweet" street, and it becomes your preferred one when you get to that juncture.

See how this works? ***We will slowly rewire your brain so that the mind manipulation path is replaced by one of your choosing. This way, you can replace a bad induced habit with a good one of your choosing.***

Do you want an example? Why not replace watching TV or being on social media with reading? It does not need to be "heavy reading" ... If you're not a convinced literature geek, reading *Love and Peace* by Tolstoy maybe is not the best replacement for "FootBook" or "InstaGraph" or a light TV program. But there are newspapers, comics, funny books, magazines etc....

And it's easier to read a quick magazine article instead of watching a TV program or going on social media, especially if it's meant to be a quick activity, and you have little time... But the chosen habit needs to be positive, good for you, and, above all, your choice and enjoyable.

Of course, unlike with methadone, sweets or nicotine in vaping, ***with this type of replacement therapy we want you to increase, not reduce, the replacement substance or better activity because it is healthy and good for you!***

Replacement Therapy Must Be Enjoyable

Let's take an example. Do you know how many people have tried to become vegetarians or vegans and failed? That was especially true in the past. Do you know why? Try stopping eating steaks and replace them with lettuce and carrots!

Once upon a time (it looks so long ago now), vegetarian and vegan food was "boring". Mind you, you will get used to tasting a leaf of lettuce, but it's very unrealistic to think that you can replace the strong sensation of eating steak with it... But vegans and vegetarians came up with new recipes, food that tastes like (even better than) meat, with the same consistency (even juicier) ... And in recent years, the number of vegetarians and vegans is in fact growing very rapidly.... In 2018, 5% of US residents were vegetarians and 3% vegan. In most European countries the number of vegetarians is even higher, usually between 7 and 11%.

But all these people had to go through replacement therapy. By having good, enjoyable, and even fun and visually attractive food makes it more achievable.

One of the great successes of vaping is that you can have all the flavors you want... That gives pleasure, and a wide range of "rewards" ... It makes it fun to try blueberry rather than chocolate... This is an advantage over tobacco, which, for though different brands may have slightly different flavors, it is always tobacco flavor...

So, if you have a problem, like, your children watch too much TV – ok, then, first of all congratulations for focusing on this. Second, what have you been thinking as a replacement? Can I give you a list to choose from?

- Board or card games

- Doing house chores
- Playing football
- Doing homework
- Playing video games
- Playing with friends in the garden

Which ones would you choose? Which wouldn't you choose? Why? See you after a pleasurable break.

...

I had to change the radio channel, the music was too "harsh" ... You see, I replaced watching TV with listening to the radio in the morning... Ok, I think we will agree that there are three we can really choose: board and card games, playing football, playing with friends in the garden. You can add as many similar ones as you wish, like playing with dolls, playing with the dog, painting, dancing etc....

The point is that *you have to replace children's TV time with something fun!* But how many parents say, "Why are you watching television? Go and do your homework!". What happens here? That they give an unpleasant alternative and negatively reinforce the TV watching habit!

This must happen millions of times every day... If only they stopped to think... If only they understood what you know now! These parents must be in perfect good faith but in many cases, they are just making the problem worse.

So, homework and house chores are not functional, but how about video games? There is a double problem with this: they are *even more addictive* than TV and they are by no means healthy.

So, now you see how the **choice of replacement needs to be healthy, enjoyable, and not highly addictive.** You now have the keys to the solution of many problems of mind manipulation.

This does not just apply to children. Adults too want to have fun; they want to enjoy themselves etc.... Apply these rules to you as well...

By the way, how has your "long term replacement experiment" been going?

...

I hope it's going well, but maybe now you know more things about how to use replacement therapy, and you want to bring some changes? Maybe you want to change the replacement? Maybe you want a more positive one? On this point, social activities are always a good choice... Is your child watching too much TV? Invite one of his/her friends over! Quick solution, healthy and gold for social skills...

Maybe you think the reward is not enough? Then...

Add Extra Rewards to the Replacement

Do you know what some people who stop smoking do? They put their cigarette money into a piggy bank, even part of it... Then, at the end of the month or so, they open the piggy bank, and they find out how much they have saved.

This is excellent! Do you realize how many things you can do with the money you spend on cigarettes? It depends on where you live, in the USA the average cost of a pack is $6.28 at the time of writing; but in some European countries it can easily get to the equivalent of $10.00! Two packs and you can go out to the restaurant. Five packs and you can buy new shoes! Imagine after an average of thirty packs in a month... what would you get? A weekend break, a small holiday?

You see, this is *extra positive reinforcement.* You can always add it "from outside". For example, if you propose playing in the garden instead of watching TV to your child, add something more... Say, "If you do this I will..." – and add something nice but positive. Don't buy them off with sweets! Something like "I will let you play with your friend tomorrow," or "I will help you with your homework," or "I will get you new crayons," etc....

The odd treat is always fine, I am not advocating a Spartan regime! But don't make it a habit of replacing a bad thing with another bad thing. Especially if you are caught unprepared, you are busy with something else etc., "I will get you an ice cream," every now and then is perfectly fine. Then good quality Italian ice cream is actually ok(ish) in terms of health...

You see, the more pleasure you introduce into de-conditioning your mind and rewiring your brain, the more successful you will be!

Planning and Structuring Replacement Therapy

Imagine your replacement therapy like a graph... You will need to increase the replacement by steps while at the same time you reduce the bad habit. One line goes up, the other goes down. And yes, going past that 50:50 point is quite important, one of the main turning points.

But how can you do this? Are there any strategies you can use? Of course, there are!

There are quite a few tricks you can use...

Choose the time to start well

People are more likely to succeed if they start replacement therapy at a relaxed time, a good time or "during a break". Stopping smoking when you change jobs, when you go on holiday, when you start a new relationship or anyway when you are not very stressed is always far more effective.

Don't expect too much too soon

Don't give yourself unfeasible, "athletic" targets, like, "I will stop eating sweets in a week," if that is your problem… No, give yourself plenty of time! Of course, this will depend on what you want to give up. Smoking is very hard, and I can say it from experience. I found not watching TV very easy for example… Yes, I have changed many habits in life…

Be flexible

Even if you want to set targets, be ready to change them. Leaving an open-end date is also possible. It depends a bit on you. If you know yourself well enough and you are aware that "open end projects are not for you" then avoid it. But if you trust that you have enough willpower and you can leave the final goal unscheduled, please do.

In any case, however, **be ready to change the timing, and even scale down the project temporarily.**

Keep in mind that life can be tough and "things happen"

Unexpected things happen in life. You may be perfectly on track one day, then the next day you get a "blow" from life... I don't wish it to you or anybody. But if it happens, just slow down, readjust, put it off... But don't give up!

Don't beat yourself up if things go wrong

And on this topic, if things go wrong, don't lay the blame on yourself. This too is mind conditioning! You see, we are taught that if we start a project and it goes wrong, it "*must*" be our fault. In some cases, ok, it's true. But in most cases, people have to give up because of unforeseen events and events that do not depend on them.

It is not your fault if the market changes. It is not your fault if a friend lets you down. It is not your fault if you fall ill. It is not your fault if you lose your job or it does not go too well. It is not your fault if your car breaks down and you need to buy a new one... Get the point?

Stopping smoking is a good example here. People have setbacks and they start again... Ok, it happens. But if they blame themselves for the setback, then they negatively reinforce their smoking habit... And no, I'm not completely saying that you shouldn't take responsibility for things that ARE in your control to just blame something else. Be mindful of this.

Start with about 5 to 10%, not more!

These percentages give you a rough idea. It's hard to quantify certain things. But for example, TV... If you watch it for 3 hours a day, start with a bit less, not half... Take away 15 minutes on day one, and then move to 30 etc.

With cigarettes there can be a double way to be honest. You can start reducing how much you smoke, by one cigarette a day (or every two or three days) and then stop altogether.

You can do it while vaping as well, but actually with vaping stopping cigarettes altogether is quite easy. Then again, you will start with high nicotine levels, then reduce it little by little. I actually started with the highest possible level of nicotine. I know myself... I know I like strong sensations... and I wanted to make sure that vaping would be stronger than smoking cigarettes. It worked. But then I cut down slowly, actually very slowly by other people's standards.

Add extra rewards at each stage

Every time you change steps, every time you achieve a partial success, every time you make progress, give yourself a treat, some extra positive reinforcement. Even thinking about it beforehand has a great, positive motivational effect: "If I cut down another cigarette, I will treat myself to a movie on Sunday…" Savor it as the moment gets nearer and your aim is getting closer. Celebrating success is vital in finding more success.

Involve others

If you can, by all means tell your family and friends you will be starting a project, no need to say, "replacement therapy". You don't even need to get into the details of mind manipulation. You can simply say, "I want to change this habit/this thing in my life," and then you can simply ask them "to be aware of it" or "give you a hand if they can".

In particular, if you have a partner, you should definitely involve him or her – if it is possible.

Reflect regularly

Every now and then, say every week, take some time off all other duties and activities and reflect on your progress. Reflection is key to success, whatever you do! Reflection needs to be done with peace and calm, not in a hurry and noisy place. It needs to have an "ameliorative purpose"; it cannot be a form of "inquisition".

It's purpose is to see what has gone well (which is positive reinforcement) and then find ways of doing even better. It is not an exercise in self-flagellation, ok?

It is simple: find a quiet place. If you want to do it with a friend, your partner etc., fine... Get a cup of tea (a glass of wine is fine, actually, red is better anyway; it relaxes you, while white wine makes you nervous), and ***brainstorm:***

- ***Three things that went well.***

- ***One thing to do, to improve, or add to your schedule and plan.***

If you have more than three good things, fine! But do not add too many improvements. One or two maximum. You can always add the others that come to your mind next week. The task needs to be feasible, or you will set yourself up to fail... One good improvement and you will focus on it very well, instead.

What's inside a word?

But I want to tease you a little bit more... Did you know that you can actually use words, rephrase them, change them so that you can change people's minds and even long held beliefs?

Chapter 7 – Neuro Linguistic Programming (NLP)

What are you using when you think? What are your thoughts made of? The answer can be complex, but on a basic level, you will agree that "words and sentences" is a viable answer. And it is. We have already said it: we use words and sentences to formulate rational thoughts.

Now, I'll ask you another question: if I could manipulate the language you use, if I could influence it, would I also influence your thoughts, or even your way of thinking? Let's meet again after a short reflection.

...

Can I try and guess what you answered? I bet you thought it is possible. Now, I'll ask you a more personal question, one which you only need to answer in your mind: when was the last time you used language to sway a friend? Or to obtain something from someone?

...

Ok, I got it... You are one of the very, very few ones who never do these things. Or are you? Are you sure you've never even used a "more convincing word" to get your way? Of course we all have and do, and it's not really problematic; there is a range of linguistic choices we can make which is all fair and honest.

But how about if this *link between language and neurological processes could be manipulated?* Or, put in a different way, *is it possible to use language to induce neurological processes and then actions in people?*

This does not need to be used in a negative way; it can be used to cure people. And in fact, this concept has been developed by some psychotherapists, including **Richard Bandler** and **John Grinder** who, in the 1970s theorized a way of treating mental issues with language, or what we call **NLP,** or **Neuro Linguistic Programming.**

Does NLP Work?

I need to start by being very straightforward with you. Many scientists believe that NLP is not actually a functional method. Let's say that for many years, there has been large opposition to the validity of this theory.

But science does and must change its mind when new discoveries and studies come along. Recent peer reviewed research has started to show that its academic fortune may be starting to change. In a long and detailed study published in the *Journal of Cognitive Neuroscience, 18:12, 2006,* we find evidence of how actual effects can be identified and traced when NLP is used, in particular, so-called "garden path effects". This is when a sentence has a meaning when in isolation, but in the context, it has a different meaning.

In any case, if you want to read more, the study is long and full of data, and it's titled 'A Neurolinguistic Model of Grammatical Construction Processing' and written by Peter Ford Dominey, Michel Hoen, and Toshio Inui.

But leaving academic debate behind, it's still quite useful that you know about this very specific field.

Now, I just discussed the academic standing of NLP for correctness. But I also need to tell you that what we mean now for NLP is not the same as what Bandler and Grinder meant. You see, they had meant it as a psychotherapeutic method. By this we mean a set of strategies and theories that a psychotherapist can use to treat and / or cure people. Despite some positive signals, as a psychotherapeutic method, it's still regarded as being based on wrong premises and not functional. But...

Developments in NLP

If NLP has not found much fortune in psychotherapy, it has found fertile ground among manipulators, especially in sales, marketing, persuasion, negotiation and similar fields. You see, the idea that you can use language to convince people is pretty self evident, unlike the idea that you can build a whole set of strategies to cure people using only language...

Soon after its announcement to the world, NLP caught the interest of marketing companies, sales agencies, business training providers and the like. They took the principles fairly, freely, and roughly, but they developed a *striking set of techniques and stages to "grab people's attention" and then convince them to change their minds and then act upon it.*

Applications of NLP

Let's meet our vacuum cleaner door to door salesman again (let's make him a man this time). Shall we give him a very trustworthy name? How about Ben? Ok, then. Ben has it all: he's well groomed, he has the gift of the glib; he's naturally pleasant, well educated etc... He still does not get great results though...

He tries and tries, but the vacuum cleaners he sells are still few and far between... So, he thinks that there is something about his speech, about his delivery, about his technique that does not work. You see, he's self critical...

So he looks around. At the time there was no internet but he found some flyers with NLP written on it... And he finds that there is an actual method, *a script in clear stages and phases that can get you from grabbing someone's attention to actually getting them to do what you want them to.*

Basically, it's a *step by step guide to "persuading" people*... "Great," he thinks to himself, "I am taking this course straight away!" He did. He paid $50.00 (back in the days it was a lot) and – you guessed – his sales increased an awful lot!

And you know what? You can now get the same course Ben took – and for free! Just read what is coming next!

...Sorry, I identified a bit too much with the course trainer... Anyway, I'll show you what these steps are... For free, of course.

Anchoring

This is the "foot in the door" stage. For Ben, it used to be a door in the face before he realized that what matters is to strike the customer with an ***immediate sense of bonding.*** And that's where Ben had been going wrong! How can you establish a connection talking about a vacuum cleaner?

Now, look at advertisements – let's say something like food for kids. You have a problem here: you need to sell food for kids to adults. Ok, you are right, some ads are directed at kids (so that they nag their parents), but many are directed directly at the parents, aren't they?

So, what can they use as anchoring?

...

You will have noticed that many ads show happy families, smiling and healthy children, a playful but very "orderly" scene... You see, this is what parents want their children to be. This is what makes parents happy.

If you compare ads targeted at children, the scene is often much more colorful, crazy, dynamic, playful, even surreal... This is because these ads anchor to their vivid imagination, not to their parents' wishes and dreams...

You see, **you need to catch the other person's attention with an image, sentence, phrase, idea that s/he likes**.

Do you want to guess what Ben did next? He switched his intro… Instead of talking about the vacuum cleaner, he started talking about "cleaning up after children". He then developed questions as if he was carrying out a survey, like, "Do you ever get your child to clean the floor?" and "Would you like to?"

You see, he worked out how to anchor his speech. **Anchoring requires an emotional engagement on behalf of the "target", the person we want to persuade.** Remember that at the time most of the people Ben met were middle class women, with children etc. So, he got the "right way in".

Belief Change

Only after Ben was sure that he had fully anchored the customer, he moved on to the second stage: belief change. In case the first anchor did not work, he tried a second, then, on rare occasions, even a third. In any case, he would **never move into the "belief change" phase if the anchor had not worked**.

And he realized a big mistake he had been making... Talking about the vacuum cleaner straight away meant trying to change the customer's belief without having made an emotional connection first.

After the course, he already knew that if the anchor had not worked, he was wasting his time. There was no way the customer would end up changing her or his mind.

And this is exactly what all his job was about, isn't it? Making people change their minds and believe they need a new vacuum cleaner. At least in 99% of cases...

How can you make people change belief? First of all, you need to believe that they can change their mind. And this is a basic tenet of NLP. If you use the right words, the right ideas, the right images, most people can be made to change their mind. The question is, however, "how?"

There are some guidelines that NLP experts use:

- *Take it slowly and in small steps.* You cannot change someone's mind in one big step... You will need to "move" the person's position very slowly. Experts actually visualize the person, and watch carefully how she or he moves, making sure that they don't revert back to their original position.

- **Ask questions.** NLP users will ask lots of questions about the issue they are focusing on. This way they get two results:

  1. They collect information about the person and his / her possible problems.
  2. They instill a sense of doubt and uncertainty within the person.

Don't forget that if I ask you a question, I force you to doubt your position. This way, I am already taking you to a position where making you change your mind is easier.

- **Offer solutions.** Offer solutions to the problems that arise from the questions. This will make you look knowledgeable and trustworthy. But also make sure that **the solutions lead to your final goal.** In Ben's case, the final goal is selling a vacuum cleaner, so, his solutions will be "masked ways of saying: you need a vacuum cleaner".

I want to give you an example here, to make it clearer. A potential customer complained that children play football every day and they come back with dirty shoes. And of course, he could have told her, "Get them to take their shoes off," instead he said, "You can change the carpet with wood flooring, but even then, cleats would scratch it," and then of course he said, "But it's so beautiful that they like sports, they are growing very healthy!" You see how he left her no real choice, but didn't even mention it by name?

- **Narrow the circle.** This is quite a haunting image. Have you ever seen hawks hunt? They start with large circles and make them smaller and smaller in the sky. Basically, they "close in on the prey". And trust me, many NLP users see it exactly in these terms.

  What Ben did about the footballers is also an example of "narrowing the circle." You basically have to show that all other options are "dead ends'' and in the end, when you offer yours, after the person has been struggling to find a solution, you will look like a hero, or heroine!

You see, it's a step by step strategy where you know the final goal, and, with well chosen questions, words etc. you close some "paths" and only leave the gates that lead to your pre-decided solution open. When the person you are trying to persuade gets there, *it must look to the person as if s/he had got to that solution freely and independently.* In reality, you led him / her there and s/he has not even realized it.

Along the way, there are also other techniques you should use. And here they are...

Reframing Content: Rephrase and Reformulate Sentences

Have you ever noticed how professional salespeople (like for insurances, cars, technical items especially) like to rephrase what you say? They don't just add a technical tone to the conversation, they do two more things this way:

- *They show you that they are the experts, not you, so you need to trust them.*

- *They put things in a way that make your perspective look better.*

Let's go back to our footballing kids. How would you rephrase, "They come in with dirty shoes and the dirt doesn't come out"?

...

Fine, this was a tricky question, First of all because you are not an expert, second because it does depend on your aim... Well, you know what Ben said before giving his "loaded solution?"

"True, grass and mud get caught in the fibers of your carpet, I see. If it's wet then you need a lot of power to get it off."

You see, he shows that he knows a lot about the problem, and he also hints that the solution is "lots of power"... Not that it's "taking those dirty cleats off..."

Also, people who want to manipulate users with NLP will rephrase verbs in a very skillful way. For example, "want", "desire", "would like" will become "need" or "can't do without". You see, this way they switch a simple "wish" to a need! Similarly, if you say, "I can't afford it," they will change it into "You could afford it if," or similar constructions.

But there is more to language in NLP techniques... There's also body language.

Mirroring

This is a common technique used by manipulators to give you a subconscious impression that there is "feeling" or that you are "both on the same wavelength". You see, psychologists and sociologists have noticed that people who really get on well together naturally coordinate their movements. Research shows that if you are fully in tune with a friend, the chances that you pick up the glass at the same time increase enormously.

And there is more; they also noticed that if people really get on well, they tend to sit in the same way, or stand in the same way. They also tend to face each other perfectly (and not lean or turn away) and sometimes they literally mirror each other's actions. Like when your friend strokes her hair and you do the same...

Now, I'll ask you a little favor. You can do it now, if you want, or later... Just take a walk where people have fun, like a park, especially where people play sports or have lots of leisure facilities. Even a movie theater is quite good. While you are there, look at couples and groups of people. Check out which ones you think get along really well together, and those who don't. What can you say about mirroring each other's actions?

...

This time I had the chance to go to a flower show! Loved it. I also noticed that there were couples there, and some would focus on the same flower. Some even touched the same plant at the same time! Others, however, were focusing on different things, one looking one way, the other the other way...

Naturally, I formed an idea in my mind: those who acted in unison seemed to be more "attuned", more in agreement with each other. I don't know if they actually were. But that's not our point. Our point is that, *when we see people mirroring each other, we assume that they are on the same wavelength.*

I bet your experience was not different from mine... Now, here is the trick... How about if, say our Ben, learned to copy his customer's actions, movements, position, posture etc.? Wouldn't he be giving his customer the impression that he is a "similar person", or "someone you can get along with easily?"

I am sure you can see how the trick works. In this respect, NLP has developed beyond pure linguistic techniques. Then again, we still call it body "language".

Synonyms Matter

We have looked at rephrasing, and this is part of it, in a way. Let's say that we have a wrong idea of what a synonym is. In fact, ask the person in the street and you will get, "Synonyms are words that mean the same," but do they?

Now, look at these synonyms and find differences between them.

- Like and love
- Work and toil
- Old and ancient
- Fresh and cold

...

I'm sure you got the point... It's very hard to find words that mean exactly the same. Most synonyms are "words within the same area of meaning but with different shades of meaning". They are "very similar", not the same...

Even words with super similar meanings have something slightly different: "choose" and "select" are very similar, but if you say "choose" you sound more friendly, more informal, if you say "select" you sound technical or, depending on the context, even "clinical and cold"... You won't tell your son or daughter, "Select the cake you want!"

This difference in meaning is the **connotation**, which is the "added meaning" we have to words. For example, "home" means a place where you can live, but the connotation is also usually of "pleasant, safe, warm, private" and similar meanings.

NLP manipulators are very good at using synonyms to shift your position very slowly. I am sure you can see how it works. If you want to move someone away from an idea, you rephrase and choose synonyms with more **negative connotations**, while if you want to "invite someone towards an idea", you will choose synonyms with **positive connotations**.

Also note that it's the **connotation of words that often carries an emotional charge.** This way, by using the emotional perception of words and ideas, it is far easier to change people's minds, rather than having to go "the rational way"...

It takes training and experience to play with words that way, but if you are worried that someone is using NLP techniques on you, sniff out the use of rephrasing and synonyms and you are on to something!

Visualization and Metaphor

A picture speaks a thousand words. Even a picture in your mind! And if a mind manipulator can manage to get the "target" to draw pictures in his or her mind, the manipulator can communicate much more effectively, vividly and convincingly.

Sometimes teachers use visualization to engage students. But you can also induce it in people. Sentences like, "Imagine a big field full of flowers in bloom," can be used to bring up visual images in people's mind.

So, our friend Ben started saying things like, "Imagine getting home and finding it spotless," or "Could you imagine if you could clean your whole living room in three minutes? Even before guests come?" You see, these images are far more effective at selling vacuum cleaners than technical descriptions, aren't they?

Metaphor, which I have added in this section is a more complex issue. We know since the times of Freud that our mind does use metaphorical language to think. In fact metaphor is so key to psychology that there are whole books written on it. Some metaphors have very deep meanings that sink into our subconscious.

Staying on the theme of home and home appliances, for example the "hearth" metaphor is very powerful. "A crackling fire in winter" brings up all sorts of connections, and of course Ben would add that with his top of the range vacuum cleaner you can clear the ashes in ten seconds afterwards. But what he is selling here is the idea of a romantic evening, or maybe a time of hugs and warmth etc...

Using metaphor means bringing up unspoken meanings in the metaphorical language used. It's like talking about something already sunk into our subconscious without mentioning it.

All you need to know to protect yourself is to **be very aware of the power of images and metaphor, and if someone uses them too much, that should ring an alarm bell.** poets excluded, of course!

The Bright Side of NLP

Don't lose faith in the Human family though! While there are people who will take advantage of anything to grift or manipulate your mind, but others have a positive outlook on life, and they can turn even very unethical and evil techniques into positive ones…

It so happens that many psychologists and other professionals have asked themselves a very deep question: "Is it possible to use NLP in a positive way?" They thought about it, tried out a few techniques and… Yes! Of course we can!

The key differences between using NLP to manipulate or even to heal are two:

- **That NLP techniques are used on a consensual person (even oneself).**

- **That NLP techniques are used for a positive goal.**

Georgina, for example, has very low self esteem. She is one of those lovely, sweet, intelligent and very gifted people who is not achieving what you would expect from life. Why? Put simply, she has a negative attitude towards achieving. She has that mindset many people have, that "things are hard to get" or even "impossible".

You know the sort of person we are talking about. People who say, "Yes, it will happen to someone else and not me," every time a positive idea comes their way.

Can I ask you a question? Now that you have learned a lot about NLP, could you see ways in which we could use it to help Georgina?

...

I suppose you have come up with a few ideas already. Maybe you thought that if we help her rephrase sentences with positive synonyms, positive verbs, strong expressions of willpower, little by little she will start building her confidence. And you would be right!

NLP is a technique to change people's attitudes and ideas, and that can also be used to change bad ideas into good ones!

How to Use NLP for Good Reasons

You can use NLP on yourself. Using positive affirmations (which we will see later in this book), is a way of changing your mindset. Visualizing positive results is another (again, look at the last chapter of this book for these techniques with practical exercises). In fact, lots of the exercises in Chapter 13 are based on NLP. But I know you are patient to wait …

Ok then, just because I am a "softie" as students say… First of all:

- **You need to know your traits well and be honest about them.** Asking a friend or significant other to be "tough but fair" with you could be a good idea. There are things that, despite all our efforts, we cannot see in ourselves. But take what s/he says as a "chance to change it", not as a critique to you.

- **You need to focus on one single trait or wrong idea at a time.** You would make a mess if you tried to change all your improvable sides together. Don't even go there, for your own sake of sanity!

- **You need to decide exactly where you want to get to.** Write it down if you need to. For example, "Now I believe I am not good at my job. I will believe that I am very good at it".

- **Make a list of "negative sentences" you regularly use**. This needs to be very long and detailed. These are the sentences that "build your thoughts in a negative way."

- **Cross them out and write positive versions of them.** You don't need to memorize them. Use these as "inspiration" and then...

- **Use every chance you have to rephrase and reframe.** This needs to be *regular and frequent.* It's fine if you sit there in the evening for 30 minutes and you look back at your day and say, "I said this and I should say that," and go through all the negative thoughts of the day.

But you must also do this with small but regular changes. Change many, short, simple sentences several times a day. Imagine a spider weaving a cobweb that catches bad thoughts... The more regular it is, the more frequent the individual threads, the better it works...

You can start now. Just make sure you keep it all positive!

For fully detailed (easy and fun) activities, please wait till Chapter 13. But now you know how to identify and defend yourself from NLP manipulators and you can even start using it for your own good.

Getting Personal

So far, we have focused on mind manipulation through the media and similar ways, but what happens if you meet someone in person who wants to manipulate you? I am not talking about the professional salesman, here... We'll get to them as well, but in due course. I am talking about that manipulative colleague of yours, or the store manager who always gets what he wants...

You know, those who do it – let's say by vocation? So, if you want to know about them and how to stop them... Well, first treat yourself to something you really enjoy, then just meet me in the next chapter...

Chapter 8 – Manipulators in Everyday Life

Have you ever worked hard only to find out that someone else got all the credit? Have you ever been tripped just in front of the finish line at a metaphorical race, at work, at school, or maybe even with friends, acquaintances etc.? I bet you have. I have. Most people have, and the exceptions are often "on the other side" of the fence in this case: they are the manipulators.

There are quite a few people who manipulate others in everyday life, especially at school and at work. "Why at school and work, especially," is the question you may be asking now? Let me tell you...

What Turns People into Manipulators

Alex is an adolescent student. His parents are quite demanding, and they expect him to be a top student... But unfortunately, while he is academically gifted, he is not "as gifted as quite a few other students in his class".

However, he finds out that a very intelligent girl, Asia, has a soft spot for him... So, he makes friends with her. He butters her up, he talks to her... Well, you know... He feeds her infatuation instead of telling her the truth, which is that he does not like her at all. But he knows he has something to get from her if he keeps flirting with her: he can get her to help him with class and homework, and, if all goes to plan, he can even get her to write his homework, essays etc....

And he manages... That goes on till he changes school, then, he starts all over again, this time with a girl called Rebecca. Then he starts work, and, well, the situation is slightly different, but the game is the same... And he finds that his colleague, Sarah has noticed his good looks...

This is a sample story, but the pattern is quite common. People learn that manipulating others is "advantageous" to themselves and they hang on to it at first as a strategy to meet standards expected from them, then they refine their technique, and they use it for "benefits" like career advancement, making money etc....

Let's make the **factors that turn people into manipulators** explicit:

- **It usually starts as a tendency at a young age.**

- *The future manipulator is often under social (family) pressure to "do better".*

- *The future manipulator may (often does) feel that s/he cannot achieve the goals put on him/her.*

- *In other cases, the future manipulator is actually encouraged to manipulate by family members instead.* These are serious cases; they often end up looking at others as "objects" and even "inferior". But these also often end up being the most skilled manipulators.

- *The future manipulator achieves positive results from his early manipulation experiences (positive reinforcement).*

- *The manipulator becomes accustomed to doing it.*

- *Manipulation becomes normal practice in his work and/or social life.*

As you can see, society is, once more to blame. *A very competitive society (at school and work) is both the "motive" of manipulators when they start and the giver of the "reward".*

This is key; really, we will never get out of this cycle if we do not change society and make it less competitive. It is because of its competitiveness that young people feel "obliged" to manipulate at first... But this is also a **society which rewards manipulators, selecting them for key, well paid, and powerful posts.**

The focus on achievement, rather than honesty, the focus on competition, rather than cooperation, that we have in our social (working, school, politics etc.) structure simply means that **manipulators have an unfair, but often huge advantage over honest people in this society.**

We "select" the least trustworthy politicians... We don't, because by the time they get their name on the ballot paper they have been selected by... party, previous political life, work success etc.... And all these are already "filters" that select ruthless people, rather than honest people.

There are due exceptions, but this is very common. In my view, it is becoming more and more common, and even more pathological and grave.

How to Spot the "Manipulator among Us"

Fine, now we know what path leads people to becoming manipulators, but is there a way of spotting them, of finding them out, of identifying them? Yes, of course there is! Put simply, *everyday life manipulators will show the same signs of manipulation as "remote distance" manipulation,* the ones we saw in Chapter 4, 'Signs and Symptoms of Mind Manipulation' like, in particular:

- *Repetition*
- *Insistence*
- *False and empty claims*
- *Elusiveness*
- *Overemphatic language*
- *Contradictory body language*

They may also display the other signs too, but at this stage the usual warning: look at the signs as a whole, one single sign is not usually enough...

But there are more, specific to face to face interaction, like:

- *Excessive friendliness;* there are people who are naturally friendly, but you also have those who don't do it naturally. And, when you start a new job, when you get into a new neighborhood etc., you may know the type of person I am referring to... The one who wants to be "first in getting your confidence" ... These people often add a bit of insistence in the way they propose

160

themselves as friends. Which leads me to the next point.

- **Willingness to skip stages in pushing your relationship to the next step;** they skip too fast from "being good acquaintances" to "being good friends". They want to get your confidence, as we said, and they often use the word "friend", "trust" etc. but out of context, in a forced way... **They want you to see them as friends even before you have done all the "routine safety checks" to regard someone as a friend.**

- **They flatter you;** being complementary to encourage you, to build your confidence is fine, but when they want to butter you up... Then there may well be a hidden agenda... This is linked to overemphatic language. If you did a good job and a colleague comes and says, "Well done," or indeed, "Good job," that's fine... But if for a decent job done you get a "I have never seen such an amazing job," or, "You are phenomenal!" then beware...

- **They are confident with asking favors;** note that they will have to test your "gullibility" (their word, not mine!) and they need to do it in stages. They won't try their big grift on you without testing the ground... They will start asking you little favors first, and check if you are "one of those who can't say no", or at least if you say "yes" easily, and/or how to get you to say yes... Beware of people who come back with the same request after you say "no" ... There can be exceptions, you may have a colleague who really needs that shift swap because of his/her child... But be careful...

- **They talk behind people's back;** this is bad behavior in any case, but **very typical of manipulators**. They do it because they want to influence ("manipulate") your social patterns. They want to decide your "enemies and allies"; they want to pitch you against their own "enemies", or they want your negative opinion on someone to come in handy when they need it... Never trust people who talk behind others backs. In the end, they may well do it behind yours.

Now, look out for these signs, because if you have a good quantity of these (and of those in Chapter 4), your new colleague may be bad news... By "good quantity" we mean:

- **Number of different signs**

- **Frequency of occurrence of each sign**

- **Level of each sign**, as each can be a small, little thing, or a big one, like asking you to pass a pencil is one thing... asking to take the slack for a mistake is another...

Now, we need to distinguish between "common manipulators" and even more dangerous individuals... Allegedly these are the greatest, most effective, most constant, most skilled, in a word, the most dangerous manipulators of all...

Psychopaths and Sociopaths

Psychopaths and sociopaths are becoming a "mainstream issue"; more and more, even non-professionals, "normal people" are realizing that our world has a major issue: *society favors the advancement of psychopaths and sociopaths.* It does it in exactly the same way as it promotes manipulators, by rewarding them, with better jobs, money, important positions in society, political power etc. And that is exactly what sociopaths and psychopaths crave most of all.

For them, these rewards, especially power and influence, control over others and money, are by far the most pleasurable rewards ever. And note that society proposes them as such, rather than happiness, health, good relationships, fun, being useful to others...

And sociopaths and psychopaths are perfectly adapted to this system of non-values and rewards for being "ruthless" rather than "honest". Why? It's in the name. *Sociopaths and psychopaths are incapable of feeling emotion and empathy for others.* This means that *they see people as objects,* or "things to use to their advantage".

Theirs is a serious condition, a disorder, that needs to be treated. They are actually dangerous to society, to people around them, and to anyone they get in contact with. And because they have no qualms, no sense of guilt, they are excellent liars and manipulators.

There are many symptoms that show you someone is a sociopath or psychopath, on top of being excellent manipulators, so, showing some/most of the signs we have seen so far...

- *They are self-centered;* their world is all about themselves. Everything that happens matters only for what it does to them.

- *They are not self-critical;* they don't admit when they are wrong; in their mind, they can only be right. *They blame mistakes on others,* and even see "conspiracies" against them when they get it horribly wrong.

- ***They show no real emotions towards others;*** they can try to fake them, but they are quite bad at that... You will notice that they "cut emotional displays short", they look "uncouth" towards other people's suffering and often don't even register that the "expected response" is one of at least faked sympathy.... They often miss the "request for empathy" from others.

Note that in many boards of directors, these are "qualities" ... If you have to fire 10,000 people, if you have to tear a village to the ground to build a polluting power plant, if you have to push your company's interests above all others (including people's suffering and livelihoods etc.) the fact that you feel nothing about others is a massive career advantage. Huge. And this has now transferred into politics too...

We will look at how to deal with non-sociopathic and non-psychopathic manipulators in a second, that is a different kettle of fish... But for now...

If you spot a sociopath or psychopath in your life, in your social or working network...

- ***Never trust a single word they say.***

- *Try to break every possible link. If you can get them out of your life altogether, even better.*

- *Don't try to be a good Samaritan and try to help them with it. Only, and I absolutely mean only professionals can deal with them.* In fact, if you try to help them, they will sniff it immediately and take advantage of it. I am not joking; I know people who have had their lives *totally ruined by sociopaths and psychopaths.*

So, **the only way to subtract you from mind manipulation from a sociopath or psychopath is to get them out of your life or at least keep them as far as possible from you.** There is no middle ground, no "solving the problem while keeping the person".

But now on to sunnier – or better "less cloudy" beaches...

Dealing with Everyday Life Manipulators

Let's see how you can counter the "intrusion into your life and freedom, or will power" from that disturbing colleague of yours that you have found out wants to manipulate you... There are a few areas you need to work on, and we will assume that you can't totally cut him or her out of your life.

But this brings up a question: would it be ok to just cut them out of your life if you can? Yes. You need no "moral doubts" about it. People who try to manipulate you not only are dangerous, but they also break ethical laws, which means that you have every right to keep them out of your life.

Is it feasible all the time though? It's hard... If we are talking about someone you meet freely, like a friend, an acquaintance etc., it is easier to say, "Bye bye, our roads part here." But with family members, colleagues or even friends within a group of friends, this is much harder to achieve.

Thankfully, there are strategies you can use, and fortunately you will get to know them right now!

Find Out What They Want

If you find out what the manipulator wants, you will start getting an advantage over him/her. Even if you don't get the exact idea, but a general one. It's like when parents know why their children are throwing a tantrum... They know they can turn the tables, don't they?

Let's go back to your colleague... What may s/he want? While it is possible that s/he may want a loan, or even to steal your partner or, even to propose to you. A deal which is actually a grift... But let us *start looking at what is most probable.* Being at work, it may have to do with his or her career, job, position or even clout in the workplace.

If where you work doesn't have many career prospects, maybe then it's not the promotion he or she wants. Maybe it's just clout, or looking good with the boss... or maybe it's a long term career prospect s/he is after. Still, there are those who seek the boss's approval, just for its own sake... Like there are those children who seek the teacher's "special approval" to be the teacher's favorite... Just as a reward in itself.

Of course, **you can use the manipulator's words, interest, frequent topics etc. to narrow down the options...** If she or he keeps talking about a particular person, area of the job, project etc., the chances are that his/her "hidden agenda" has to do with these.

Give Conflicting Signals

Yes, you got that right. It's not unethical, because you are doing it to protect yourself, and because these signals need to be about what s/he wants to know from you without your consent. If people ask you about your private business, is it ethical to lie? Absolutely yes! They have no right to know it and you could just tell them to mind their business. But that can be taken as rude and turned against you... So, what can you do? Tell them something wrong which in any case they should not be interested in, and should not have asked.

The same principle applies when manipulators are testing the ground... Let's see a couple of common examples. Imagine you work out that a colleague is testing your ability to say no and willingness to do favors. Let's say you are actually inclined to do favors, you like it. But you know that if s/he finds out how to get a favor from you, the manipulator may use it against you...

So, sometimes say, "Yes of course," as if it's what you'd love to do... Other times say, "No, I can't," maybe giving no explanation at all. Then spice it all up with, "Maybe, but why did you say you needed it?"

If you don't show the manipulator what makes you do things, she or he will not make the final move, the one that's meant to grift you, trap you, cheat you, trick you, whatever it is s/he wants...

Another example is when they seek your allegiance. You know those people who, maybe during meetings, or in any case in front of other people, call you into question to back them up? Manipulators do it a lot; only, they also use the people they involve this way as scapegoats if things go wrong...

Imagine the manipulator has a project, like selling a new brand of shoes (let's imagine we work in a store). S/he needs support when proposing it to the store manager. S/he talks to you about it. In front of the manager s/he calls on you and even makes you express an agreement which is beyond what you had told him/her... You may have noticed this tactic...

Then the manager says, "Ok, it looks good, let's try it!" The new brand of shoes come, they're poor quality, they don't sell, and... you find out that in a private meeting, the manipulator tells the manager that it was your idea and s/he only voiced your view because you are too shy... Thank you very much!

Here, then two things:

- ***Never allow the manipulator to claim the consent or agreement you actually did not give.*** Don't be shy and don't think about saving his/her face in front of the boss when s/he says that you "agreed fully" while you only mumbled a half-hearted "ok". S/he would not think twice about throwing you under the bus if necessary. Say it politely, but say, "Actually I only said it looked ok as a general idea/at first glance, but it needs looking into..."

- **On a one-to-one basis, give positive and negative views over his or her plan.** Sometimes say, "It could work," other times express doubts. Be critical, without being unreasonable. Do it especially as the manipulator is discussing the plan with you...

On this point, the conflicting signals can work on many levels. If s/he pays you a compliment, smile once and don't smile next time. If s/he says, "Can I get you a coffee," say yes once and, "No, coffee is bad for you," next time...

Without looking deranged **you need to avoid giving him/her the certainty that you will react as s/he expects you to when the "moment" comes.**

In the end, keep this maxim in mind: **manipulative people are also calculative people: muck up their calculations then!**

Don't Reward Flattery

One thing is a well-intentioned compliment, another is flattery. Manipulative people will flatter you till you are useful to their ends. And the more you respond positively, the more they will identify you as "an object to manipulate". So, cut it off as soon as possible.

When your now infamous colleague says, "You are the best in this office/store/job/class etc.," don't smile and blush shyly... Just say, "No, actually there are many great people here," or even better, ignore him/her... which leads me to the next point.

Ignore the Manipulator as Much as Possible

Giving no reply to manipulators means giving no feedback, which they cannot use either way. Imagine what Skinner would have done if the little mouse in the torture chamber (sorry, "Skinner box" as they call it) had not responded to the loudspeaker at all? Just because I know it was long ago, the loudspeaker told the mouse to pull the lever, the lights what the result would be, food or electric shock...

I don't know if he would have been disappointed, confused, upset... I know he could not have worked out how the little mouse thought and reacted to his stimuli. And manipulators see us a bit like mice to analyze and experiment with.

Plus, *the more you ignore manipulators, the sooner they leave you alone.*

Avoid Any Type of Confrontation with the Manipulator

You may wish to confront the manipulator, and tell him (her) in the face that you disagree with what s/he is doing… Don't! You will not really change the manipulator's mind, and you will obtain nothing – actually…

You may end up making things worse. Manipulators (and sociopaths and psychopaths) are usually very vindictive. They may play a role in front of you, they may even pretend to be coming towards you, to have changed their mind, they may even say "sorry." But many of them will start planning their revenge against you the moment you confront them.

This will be especially true if you do it in front of other people. Loss of face is something most of them cannot tolerate.

Alternatively, they may well use the incident to manipulate you even more. They may use it to gain your confidence, to show you that they are now reliable and then, when you least expect it… you've gotten yourself in a nightmare situation.

Get the Manipulator to Understand You Know What Sort of Person S/He Is

Having said this, there are ways of at least dropping the hint, even better, the doubt, that you know what they are up to. Avoid any direct confrontation, avoid any overt (and especially public) expression of what you know. And also avoid "teasing" sentences and words about it.

But just show, especially with behavior, that you have lost trust in the person. You may notice that the manipulator will start asking you probing questions aimed to ferret out what you know about him/her or his/her plans... And guess what?

Do not reply to them. Don't give anything away. Just leave the manipulator in doubt. That will be enough to find you "unsafe as a victim" and you should notice less ill intended "interest" in you.

Involve Significant Others and Get Their Viewpoint

Don't isolate yourself, never! While you should not "go public" at work about it, you should *talk to at least one friend or family member about it*. If you have a friend in the workplace, they would be fine too. But avoid the "colleague you know superficially" if possible.

You need to be quite honest about the manipulator with your confidant, and you need to **talk regularly about what the manipulator is doing.** At the very least every week.

Very importantly, **listen to what your friend or family member has to say; s/he may have a very insightful viewpoint, thanks to his/her internal perspective.** When you are in the middle of something, it's hard to see exactly what is happening to you, isn't it?

Also, **keep track of changes and improvements together.** It will be a developing situation, so it's easy to lose track of how things were, compared with now. Instead, you need to see if and how much the manipulator is giving up. But you also need to be aware of new, maybe intensified "heights"; the stronger and more frequent they are, the more likely it is that you are moving back into the core of his/her plan, or even that the plan is reaching a climax, reaching its "final sprint".

Don't Give the Manipulator Any Money

And finally, don't give manipulators any money. Even those who are not currently bothering you. Why? It's like an invitation to start manipulating you. Even if they ask for little loans etc.... Just say "no". They know that if you are willing to part with your money you are most likely a trusty person, and that plays in their hands.

What is more, in many cases, the final aim is money or money related, and, even if not all manipulators are sociopaths or psychopaths, loads of them see money as the ultimate reward, or a very pleasurable one anyway.

From Skinner's Box to "the Box"

Ok, I pushed it a bit... "The box" is an old-fashioned way of calling the television... But this is exactly what we are going to see next: how the television manipulates the masses, and how you can protect yourself from that "Big Brother" in your living room...

Chapter 9 – Mind Manipulation on Television

I switched off my TV in 2012, and I never regretted it. Actually, it's possibly one of the best things I have done in my life. "Don't you miss it," you may ask? Not at all! "How do you get the news?" I get it from other outlets, and I get more, better quality and a wider range.. I now actually get information on all the things that TV news doesn't tell you. In the end, you can change as many channels as you want, there will be different spins on the same news items. But the news items are basically always the same.

TV News and "Spin"

Do you know how much of what you get on TV is "commentary" or better "spin" on a news item and how much is the news item itself? The vast majority is all "commentary", depending on the item etc., but always far above 50%, usually more than 70% and in very controversial cases, like important topics, even past 90%.

But what is actually the function of commentary? Once upon a time it was meant to explain, and give different viewpoints. In a very small part, it is still so, but *most commentaries on TV are meant to "convince you" of a spin, of an opinion, of a point of view: they are mind manipulation.*

In the time you watch the TV news on TV you can actually get 2 to 4 times as many different items on other media! All you need to do is avoid all the "commentaries". But do you like actual commentaries? Have you noticed on TV that:

- *You cannot choose a commentary on a topic you want to develop,* they do it for you, they tell you what should matter to you.

- *Most commentaries are useless arguments between two so-called experts, or political rivals.* These don't actually add any in depth development or exploration of an issue or topic; they are just two people vying for your allegiance; this too is mind manipulation.

You can find in depth commentaries online, read them in the newspapers, on blogs etc. And you can *choose the ones that interest you.* This very choosing puts you *in control of what you read, listen to, or watch.* You see, a key *strategy to stop mind manipulation though the media is to become "free" from the media themselves.*

Now, most people watch more than one TV news bulletin a day... Do you? If you do, are the items different in the various bulletins over the day? Think about it.

...

You will see that part of the morning bulletin is repeated in the midday bulletin, then by far most of the dinnertime show is the same as the midday one, and at night there is virtually no change at all. So, what you get is *repetition of the same items with the same viewpoints, commentaries, and spin.* And as you will remember, repetition is a key mind manipulation strategy.

But then, how much do people actually remember of news bulletins? What do they remember most? Use your experience, think about friends, family, acquaintances, colleagues... what do you think?

...

The fact that people forget the news is common knowledge. Sometimes it goes too fast, sometimes people don't get it perfectly well to start with, very often the memory deceives us. You must have noticed the colleague or family member who gets the facts wrong when "repeating the news" to you...

But there is more... Here though, note that I am not advocating becoming addicted to social media, we will get to them soon, as promised.... But a recent study shows that people remember the news better if they read it online. And this is for the young and old alike.

It appeared in *Cognitive Research: Principles and Implications,* Nov 11, 2020, it's entitled 'Reading the News on Twitter: Source and item memory for social media in younger and older adults' and it's by a team of scholars, Kimberley A. Bourne, Sarah C. Boland, Grace C. Arnold, and Jennifer H. Coane.

It found out that young adults will recall the news *almost twice as well* if they read it online than if they watch on TV for example, while the difference is much lower for older adults. But here we are not advocating the use of social media as a source of news. There are many issues with this, for example, as it says, "the blending of news sources might make it harder to distinguish between news and social media". This phenomenon has reached worrying levels today; people confuse "gossip" with "fact".

What we are saying is that a significant part of what people see on the news gets lost... So... to recap:

- *Watching the news on TV is repetitive.*

- *Most of the time is spent on spin.*

- *We forget a large part of what we hear.*

Isn't it a waste of time? And why should you waste your time being told what to think and taught how to think?

But at this stage, *I am not suggesting to stop watching TV news all of a sudden.* That can actually be counterproductive. You see, lots, but really lots of what is online is mind manipulation too. Especially on some media, like "FateBook" etc. In fact, you will need to read the chapter on social media to understand how to avoid mind manipulation online. But...

You can start by watching the news only once a day, and choosing a "fairly reliable" channel. Plus...

After the news, make a (mental or written) list of the facts. This will help you remember them better, distinguish them from the spin and then you won't need "reminding" with another mind manipulating bulletin.

For the time being, stick to these two measures. We will look soon at what shows that media outlets are reliable or not... For now, I will trust your judgement.

An Alternative to TV News

The best alternative is newspapers, even online ones. Again, not all newspapers are reliable. *By all means avoid sensationalist newspapers, magazines, posts and even news channels.*

Imagine a friend of yours runs to you, all sweated, panting, with a very worried face, arms in the air and says: "Hurry up! Something terrible has happened!" What would you do? You would start running with him/her, and maybe s/he will explain what's happened on the way. But you are already:

- Worried
- Irrational
- Running
- Doing something before you actually know what has really happened.

This is the exact effect of sensationalism. *Sensationalism prevents rational thinking, creates a false sense of danger and urges you to act before you actually understand what is going on.*

Beware – I repeat – beware of anyone who uses this strategy: this is pure mind manipulation.

Choose newspapers that focus on facts, that avoid over-emphatic language, big titles with sensational and swiping statements. If you see that the article says something that then is different from the title, beware.

If you want to avoid being manipulated, you need to keep selective standards and expect very high standards when it comes to the outlets you choose.

It is possible to watch newsreels as well as in depth shows and insights online, but here too, you must choose very good ones, or you will end up from one form of manipulation to another. So, wait till we get to the social media and internet chapter.

TV and Social Media

There is a difference between what you get on TV and what you get on social media: some social media have no limits with their mind manipulation. There are people who shout like they are possessed, there are people who say the most unacceptable things, people who support the most unethical ideologies, people who give the most improbable thesis as "facts" and people who spread fake news.

So, I need to warn you: *swapping the TV for social media can be very risky; you may be exposed to forms of mind manipulation which are extreme.*

But these are good sources, we will learn to recognize them soon (ok, we have started a bit already).

Some TV channels have become more and more similar to what you get on certain vlogs and online broadcasts: extreme, angry, extremist, ready to defend any untenable concept etc. But they still have a "modicum of restraint" compared with some of the things you get online.

On the other hand, the scientific studies I quote are not available on TV… I can't even find them in my local library; I can only find them online. You see, online you have both extremes: the hard facts, parliamentary records, scientific studies, etc.… And total and utter mind conditioning trash.

The latter appeals more easily and TV channels in general have moved that way, not towards the wealth of facts, figures, and beautiful ideas you can find on the net…

That's sad, and a change of tide will only happen when we, *the people,* expect better from broadcasters.

The Quality of TV Programs

There is general consensus that TV programs have worsened in the recent decades. We can take the oldest, the most influential, the "best quality" broadcaster in the world as an example: the "mother of all televisions": the BBC.

The BBC has reduced its world-famous documentaries, its comedy and satire production (world famous too), and it has cut its "world service" which was mainly fairly factual news. At the same time, other channels have proliferated, and are mostly based on really sensationalist and low-level programs.

The advent of so-called "reality TV" has lowered the quality of TV productions consistently, over time and significantly. I have no doubts in my view that there has been some intention behind this move towards sensationalism. Sensationalism costs less, in theory gets more views (even if that is not true – over time viewers all over the Western World have been decreasing in most counties as a proportion of the population). But sensationalism is also strong mind manipulation.

We just need to look at the history of tabloids (sensationalist "newspaper") to see that there is a scientific plan to manipulate people's minds behind them... And televisions followed the same pattern, at some distance.

So, most of the programs are really a waste of time. And the other programs? Like *documentaries*, *films etc.? You can get them somewhere else; choose a platform where you can choose (!!!) which ones you want to watch!*

By now you will have understood that *real choice, personal and free choice is an antidote against mind manipulation.*

Cutting Down on Time in Front of the TV

So, we have cut down from three TV news bulletins to one. We can replace most evening and night programs with movies, series etc. we can choose on another platform... And that is actually much better... Trust me; I watch the movies that I like, not the ones that some manager in a room hundreds of miles away chooses for me. And I am picky. But I am enjoying myself much more!

So... what are we left with? Maximum one hour of TV a day? Now, my question... How many hours do you spend in front of the TV? How many hours do people spend on average?

...

I spend none, I don't know how many hours you spend a day, but the average US adult spends *more than four hours a day watching TV.* That's a lot...

Now, what do you really get from those four hours apart from very little factual information you can get somewhere else? Ok, a good dose of mind manipulation free of charge (oops, no – they actually even charge you for it!)

Cutting down to one hour, how many things could you do instead? **With three extra hours at your disposal every day!** Make a little list please.

...

So, when I said, "Take up a sport or hobby" you might have thought, "I have no time though." Well now you have three hours a day, enough to become a professional agonist, or do other things, including having quality time with friends and family, having that famous "social life" we all complain we don't have, but then we don't give up a bit of TV trash to go out and have *real* fun...

By the way, as a note, US adults also spend another 3 hours and 18 minutes on social media... Can you see how much time we can free up if we break our TV and social media addiction? Can you see why I am by no means missing the old television?

But there is more...

TV Commercials

No need to say that **TV commercials are very effective,** because of the "moving picture" quality of the ads (and other reasons we will see). They are in fact much more effective than commercials in newspapers, magazines, etc. The very quality of the commercials makes them powerful means of mind manipulation. They look great at times, some, to be honest are actually very artistic. But remember that they are not "for you" they are "against your will" and their only function is to "bend your will and manipulate your mind". In fact, for those who commission them, sign them and broadcast them to you, who are not even a "customer", but a "target". Words do matter!

Anyway, we already said that **even if you are distracted, TV ads still have a powerful and subconscious effect on you.** In fact, starting a chat or putting the kettle on while watching commercials may well be even *worse than watching them intently.* Remember, your conscious mind is the one that defends you from mind manipulation!

But the big question is: how long do we actually spend watching commercials on TV? *On average, 25% of TV time is dedicated to commercials, that is 15 minutes every hour.* Good channels reduce this to 11 minutes. In some European countries, state channels go below this.

Considering the average US adult spends 4 hours in front of the TV every day, this means *one hour being repeatedly and insistently manipulated into*

being a consumer and buying something. Then of course there are all the other aspects of mind conditioning in ads, like:

- ***Conforming to some social "values", like being "cool", rich, slim, well dressed, showing off, being "masculine" ...*** These are what we call "non values" or "false values"; real values are being good, being generous, helping others etc.... Not really promoted in commercials, are they?

- ***Becoming dependent on having, not being.***

- ***Feeling the social pressure of "keeping up with the Joneses" (peer pressure).***

Now, one hour a day is 365 hours a year, that is more than 15 full days (and nights) spent being mind conditioned. That's about the same as Alex DeLarge gets in terms of mind conditioning in *A Clockwise Orange!* Every year, to you, your family, your children!!!

And the worst is still to come!

Television and Alpha Waves

When was the last time you fell asleep in front of the television? I hope it was long ago, because you know quite well that it's not good for you. When you wake up, you feel hazed, tired (weird, you should be more relaxed and awake), sloppy, even "bloated", "feverish" and you may even have a headache...

That should ring a bell, and a worrying one at that! What's so special about the television that makes us feel so weird? Why do we fall asleep so easily in front of it, but we become more tired?

The answer is simple and scientific: *televisions send images in alpha waves.* This is a wavelength, and one that has an effect on our brain and our mind.

You see, we don't always function at the same wavelength... *When our minds are almost switched off, it works in alpha wavelength.* At this stage, we are at the *lowest level of thinking while still awake.* Below that, there is unconsciousness. But as you know, at this level, *rational and critical thinking are switched off, and we have no defenses against mind manipulation.*

Our mind in fact has different wavelengths according to the activity it needs to do:

- The higher is **gamma**: this is when we are very functional, rational, focused, in "problem solving" mode.

- Just below, there is **beta:** a mind in beta waves is busy and active, but it is not on a "mental high speed highway" ... like in gamma.

- The lowest waking wavelength is **alpha:** this is restful, when we are relaxing. In Nature, this is quite good; the problem starts when you receive *loads of stimuli (and reinforcement) during this phase.* You see, at alpha wave level our mind should have little or no focus and a calm, relaxing, "empty of stimuli" environment. Like if you are on a beach listening to the waves.

  It is not capable of dealing with many stimuli at this wavelength. You see then what television does? *It lowers your defenses, puts it in a wavelength where you cannot cope with much stimuli, with information etc. and then bombards you with instructions, ideas, opinions etc....* This is pure mind manipulation. At a very high level and on a colossally gargantuan scale!

- Lower than alpha waves there are *theta* waves; these are the ones we are in during periods of drowsiness, when we are falling to sleep, like during the hypnagogic phase.

- The lowest waves are **delta;** here we are sleeping and dreaming.

Now, if you fall asleep in front of the television, its alpha waves will also **prevent or refrain your mind from going into delta waves**; this is why then you wake up feeling tired and not relaxed. And we all understand that "TV sleeping" is not at all like "proper sleep".

People compare being under the influence of TV alpha waves to "being under hypnosis". In the "common" sense, the popular concept of hypnosis, it is fair to say so. You have no willpower, and they are telling you what to do.

From a psychological perspective however, it is different. But it is **worse!** Apart from the fact that hypnotists have deontological (ethical) rules, like doctors etc.… Then when you are hypnotized, you are in *theta waves*… just to be precise on technical issues.

So…

Cut Down on Television Time…

… and only select positive and good quality programs and channels! I think I have convinced you that it's a wise step, and that for almost a century now (70 years or so, depending on where you live) **television has been the biggest, most widespread** *and most powerful instrument of mass mind conditioning in the whole world.*

You will literally feel free, and you will feel like you are taking control of your life if you cut down on TV time, and your day will look like it has twice as many hours in it!

But careful, during those hours you will get back to yourself, be careful. Of course, don't take to social media as a replacement. But mind your door too! There are professional mind manipulators who go round ringing people's bells all day long! And no, I am not talking about some strange looking and oddly dressed "exotic" man... Most likely he will come in a suit and tie, wear a smile, and even a badge... I am talking about salespeople... next...

Chapter 10 – The Professional Salesperson

"Ring, riiiiiing!" the doorbell goes, you go to the door, open it and there he is, the professional salesman in a suit and tie and a new vacuum cleaner, better than the one you bought last year, and before you can say, "No thanks," he has started his spiel and...

...An hour later, you have bought this new wonder of technology that looks oddly similar to the one you got last year. But that one, despite all the promises showed some flaws that are getting on your nerves, long after you paid for it, of course, so, second time lucky?

Then last time it was a woman, now it's a man... And you already try justifying to yourself a choice that deep down, after the intoxication, you are starting to doubt.

Ok, no one rings doorbells with vacuum cleaners anymore. But I wanted to remind older readers of a classic door to door salesperson from years ago – "where it all started" sort of thing... To be correct, they were mostly men, few women actually did that job... Still...

From Old Fashioned Door to Door Salespeople to Today's Professionals

Things have changed. Of course they have, but in this field, there has been developments; there has been an evolution of the same techniques; they have become more powerful, more exact, but there has not been a "revolution" in the methods.

The revolution has come in the means, actually in the mediums (media, the Greek plural of medium, comes from this). *Face to face sales are now fewer, and when you finally meet the salesperson, it's often after a long process of mind manipulation that started, maybe, with an email, a post on social media, a commercial or a flyer...*

"Good," you may think, "fewer of them around!" From one point of view, true. From another point of view, it means that *you have already been pre-selected, and this makes the salesperson's job easier!*

Not so happy now? You see, the old-fashioned door to door salesperson had a tough job on her or his hands... But hold on, let's look at why most were men...

They were men because society was still broadly composed of families where the husband worked, and the wife stayed at home. That meant that most workers were men, but also that most potential customers were women...

What is more, they were always well groomed and dressed as we said, that already made them look "respectable" and "reliable". This makes a star contrast with many street and door to door salespeople from the past in many European countries: these were traveling salespeople, gypsies etc. They would not present themselves as "well adapted to the dominant society" even as "businesspeople", but as outsiders.

Now, look at the suit and tie... Would you expect that on a baker? On a fishmonger? On a grocer? No... They "dressed up" to look even more professional than other sellers...

And that's a clue; that's not changed. They look like members of the board of directors of the vacuum cleaner factory, instead they are hierarchically some of the lowest on the company's ladder...

And that's a first lie. But it also does mean that they will appeal more to people who trust the mainstream system. Unfortunately, we are all trained to do it; we are trained when we go to the shopping mall, we are trained when we watch TV etc. Few people now prefer someone dressed as a farmer to sell them grocers! And this is especially true in urban and "Westernized" societies.

Anyway, we have had a quick look at the looks, now, let's see how they speak... I used the word "spiel" but they would call it "pitch" now. Once it was basically a sentence they repeated by heart, and they still do it, especially with cold calls (which too derive from the old door to door salesperson). But experienced ones now change it a bit, they "pitch" it to you. *They will notice something you like and bring it into the conversation...*

And this leads us to a point, on how to recognize them and take control against them.

Look at Their Eyes

When professional manipulators are talking to you, *they will look around you and at what you are wearing, what you look like*. They will cast little glances here and there... Why? They are studying you. They are *looking for information about you and your life to use against you.*

They won't use it negatively; they won't blackmail you... But they will try to *endear you and win your trust by faking empathy with you.*

For example, if they see a picture of you and your children on the mantelpiece, they may use it to "soften your barriers" and talk about how children love their product. If they see you playing baseball, they will claim they love and play baseball too. So, you feel that they are "like you", the "sort of person you would be friends with".

This is only a *pitch*; they will say they love baseball even if they loathe it. But in order to use these clues to gain your trust, they need to analyze you and your environment.

But do not confuse the normal glance to the side to the inquisitive looking around. We normally look to the side when talking to others; it's very hard to hold eye contact for long periods of time. I personally look out of windows and look for green spaces when I talk... But you can notice a difference between the natural eye movement and the directed eye movement...

You need to be very experienced to read eye movements on people, but let's say that a salesperson or in any case a manipulator most likely looks away in search for details, not to release the intensity of eye contact.

If you look at the focus of their eyes, the friend who glances away is "receptive and unfocused" vaguely like staring in the distance, or at the emptiness as we say. You will on the other hand notice that the manipulator is in fact focusing quickly on an object, and actual physical detail... That's how you spot them...

But of course, there is another point that follows from this.

Don't Let Them into Your Home and Keep them in an Emotionally Neutral Place

You guessed it; if I came into your living room, how many details and facts about your life, your social relationships, what you like, your family, your jobs, etc. could I find? Look around you (even mentally if you are not there) and make a list in 30 seconds...

...

You are right, this was the shortest spot of gardening ever for me! Jokes aside... I bet you found loads. I didn't go out really, I glanced to the side and saw a little African wood statue; just from this detail, how many things can you find out about me? Try it...

...

Done? You can say a few things about me already, and yet you have not even seen my living room... For example:

- I love art
- I love handcrafts
- I love woodwork

- I like colors
- I appreciate cultures different from mine
- I am fine with helping street salespeople (that comes from a market stall, it's not something you find in stores and if you knew more about where I live you would know that there are poor people selling these things in the streets...)

All of these would not be far off the mark...

If you really have to talk to these people (maybe for work), then **choose an emotionally neutral place.** A street is fine, a public place, a bar or coffee bar etc. **The more they know about your life the more they will be able to manipulate you.**

And on this point...

Elude Questions

The manipulator will ask what seem like innocent questions; but they are not! "Did you watch the news last night?" or "Do you like traveling?" or "Did you like the last episode of Celebrity Window Cleaners?" ... Don't be fooled by them. They may look innocent, but the're not. The salesperson is trying to find out things about you to use them later to gain your trust.

Fend these questions off with no replies if possible, dismissive ones, or even ludicrous ones, like, "Let's stick to the business at hand," or "I don't care either way," or "No, but I had Marlon Brando round to mow my lawn!"

Show them that you are not willing to give them any insight into your life. This alone will tell them that you may not be worth the effort and deter them, at least partially...

Following this train of thought...

Keep Them at a Physical Distance

It's not just "keeping them out of your private life" that deters them. You can also *keep them out of your personal and social space.*

You won't need a measuring tape for this, but keep these distances in mind, and use these measures as rough guidelines:

- *Never allow the manipulator or salesperson closer to you than 1.5 feet (45 cm).* within that radius you have your *intimate zone.*

- *Try to push the manipulator to the margins of your personal zone (1.5 to 5 feet, or 45 cm to 150 cm).* Move away, move back, try to draw an "invisible demarcation line" between you two, and try to get as far as possible towards (and over) the 5 feet mark (1.5 meters).

- **If possible, push the manipulator over the 5-foot mark (1.5 meters); that is the so-called "social sphere".** If you manage this, the manipulator will feel "outside the negotiating zone", pushed back with the "general public and passersby's" then s/he will try to get back into your personal zone. Don't fall for it; resist and push back... After a while, the penny will drop, and the manipulator should understand that you "are not game".

Keeping physical distance is a powerful way of "deflecting" the manipulator's attempts at "gaining access to your personal space and trust".

But how about touching?

Be "Cruel" with Your Handshake

Usually, the only allowed form of touching between strangers is the handshake... Use it to "assert yourself" and to give a sign that you are "closed to business". How?

Simply:

- **Give a strong, firm handshake.** Avoid any softness and squeeze quite hard (without hurting). Pretend you are squeezing a lemon!

- **Be quick and leave the handshake before the manipulator does.** This will trick him or her quite badly... If you stop early the message you give is that you do not trust the person you are shaking hands with.

The manipulator will pick up these signs and signals. The better educated and experienced the manipulator may actually pick up these signals consciously and rationally. But even if s/he does not, you will still pass them on to his or her subconscious, and that can have great results in terms of demotivating him or her.

You do want to demotivate the manipulator, and one way of doing this is to show that you are not interested. But there are other ways too.

Demotivate the Manipulator

We have seen one way of demotivating, which then translates into many acts: *showing that you are not interested.* But there is another way: ***indicate that you are not capable.*** I'll give you an example...

A salesperson is trying to sell you a cable TV contract... Show this person that you simply cannot afford it. Complain about money if you wish. Say that you are facing sudden and unexpected expenses, whatever is necessary to give the signal that ***whatever the manipulator says or does, you are simply in no position to comply.***

A salesperson is trying to sell you a holiday? Say you are not taking time off work this year! Someone is trying to get you an even cheaper utility contract? Say that you cannot do it without your partner. "And when will you be able to talk about it to your partner?" is the obvious question. "S/he is away at the moment; s/he won't be back for at least a week."

That means, "Call back if you care in 10 days, and you know that I won't answer..." Which leads us straight into another tactic you can use...

Kick It into the Long Grass

Say you cannot take any decision. The manipulator will ask you "when" of course, and you need to:

- **Be vague on the time.** Give an approximate number of days, weeks etc. There's a huge difference between saying, "On Friday," and "In at least a week." The first gives an appointment ready to schedule. The second says, "Not sure," and it also asks the manipulator to count the days. This shows that you are not collaborating... But there is more... If the manipulator calls and it's too soon, as you haven't given an exact number, s/he will know that s/he will have basically spoilt all her/his chances... Use it on them!

- **"I will not know until..."** This formula puts a condition in the future. "I will not know until I check with my boss," you could say at a business meeting. Or "I will not know until my daughter tells me which school she likes to go to..." You see, adding conditions that cannot be established now makes the manipulator understand that there is no chance of immediate success. It delays things but it also means that the manipulator needs to invest extra efforts for a result s/he thought s/he would get straight away... That may make them reconsider and realize that you are not worth their time...

- **Change medium...** "How will I know if your daughter has decided," asks the manipulator... "You can send me a text message," should be your answer, not, "Come and see me later…" Show that your preferred method is not face-to-face, but distant communication. That already is a massive blow to their plans. Then, of course, don't answer the text message and if you can, even block the number… That should pass the message on, and with the least possible risk and stress on your behalf.

Even this method follows the idea of *"putting a distance between you and the manipulator."* But there are even more ways you can use, including what comes next.

Ask for a Written Document, Agreement or Contract

This is also useful for cold phone calls and other marketing strategies. My father gets an awful lot of those. Excuse me the digression, but they know he is one of those who likes to change his utilities providers… That's a little trap by the way… The more often you change your electricity company, the more others know you do and try to contact you and get you to change again…

Anyway, my Mum always tells him, "Get them to send you a written proposal!" You know what, even with these "reliable official big companies" in most cases the proposal never comes through the post. Why? They know that **one thing is listening to, or even hearing terms and conditions, another is reading them...**

Manipulators will not usually like to put things down in writing because:

- **You can read a written document when you want, with calm and, above all, in their absence.**

- **You can read a written document with someone else, or show it to them.**

- **It is easier to pretend that they respect a contract if it is written.**

This does not mean that they will absolutely deny you a written document. I find that especially with online sales, the trend is that if you ask for one you get a very improper answer, however: "No, we can only make this offer on the phone," which to my knowledge is actually illegal in all the EU and many other countries.

They may even have a contract but avoid it at all costs.

Don't Allow Manipulators to Hurry You When Reading a Document

They will give you a text, which often is long, written in small print, hard to read, and *they will insist on you signing it as soon as possible, in a hurry. Absolutely never do this!*

Take the contract home, read it calmly, check every detail, discuss it with your partner, family, friends and for anything really worth a lot, show it to a lawyer! Take your time and beware of offers that expire soon... There will be others. One of the reasons for these offers (which look a bit like the offers at a department store, by the way... not by chance, we take them lightly because unfortunately we have been "trained" to do so).

Very often, these offers are perfectly fine at the beginning... They have written in big letters something like "99c a month!" and it's true. For the first few months. But in the small print, they have something that reads like "We reserve the right to alter the offer without notice". And guess what? You have 60 days to cancel the contract and on day 90 the 99c starts going up... First, it's $1.50, then $2.00 then $3.00 and at the end of the year the average is higher than the cellphone contract you had before.

In the end, ask yourself a question: **why would an honest negotiator hurry you into signing something?** If I am confident about the value of my offer, I would actually be happy for you to take your time and see how good it is, no?

There is a famous law in negotiations, well known by governments and big business: **in a negotiation, the negotiator who is pressed for time is at a serious disadvantage.** If a company has a strong need to clench a deal by a certain time, they will never want the company they are dealing with to know it. The reason is that this company would push the deal to the very end, and then get the hurried company to sign any bad deal.

Don't let manipulators put you into this position. Always claim all the time you need. What is more **beware of any words, sentences and signs that try to put you in a hurry.**

I usually say, "No, if you are trying to hurry me *by principle,* I stop all dealings immediately, sorry," at the very first sign of pressure.

Don't Lad Them On

And finally, don't be tempted to lead them on... I know the temptation... Sometimes we want to play, even play cat and mouse... But really, these are professionals, and they always have great advantages over you.

Think that your time will be better spent reading a book, watching a movie, playing with your children or even doing the washing up, really... ***Any sign of interest will be taken as a sign of your weakness.***

So, while you may be thinking that you are playing the cat, you are actually the mouse. They are actually studying you systematically and, even if you don't buy the now notorious vacuum cleaners, they will still get something from you. Guess what?

You think it's just your time? No, have you got a picture of young children? Fine, you will get someone ringing the bell, and, Ring, riiiiiing!" the doorbell goes, you go to the door, open it and there he is, the professional salesman in a suit and tie and a new *stroller for your baby*, better than the one you bought last year, and before you can say, "No thanks," he has started his spiel again.

You see, they can still make their time worthwhile by collecting information on you and literally selling it to another company, another salesperson that wants to sell you something, yet another manipulator...

Of course, the best option is always to "shut the door in their faces" and these are strategies to use if you can't do that (straight away). But there are ways of getting past your door anyway, and there are manipulators that you will find harder to shut out... And you will find them in hordes, on the various "InstaGross", "FootBook" and "TelePost" ... Yes, and now on the notorious social media, up next...

Chapter 11 – Social Media: The Last Frontier of Mass Manipulation

Take a mental picture of a busy street about 20 years ago. Then take another mental picture of the same street, with the same number of people, on a similar day – but recent. Take a picture of a table, at a café, or restaurant 20 years ago, with people having fun. Wind forward 20 years. What's the main difference you notice?

Clothes have changed little in 20 years (fashion has not moved much forward), hairdos have changed a bit more. But the big difference will definitely be smartphones. Loads of them. Virtually always in almost everybody's hand. And with smartphones come those tiny colorful icons of letters, birds, and other symbols: social media!

Do you remember a time when social media did not exist? Do you remember what you did instead? Do you remember how your life was different? Some of us do, the older generation. But younger people have been brought up in a world already "packaged" with social media. I'm not sure that the social media are actually the ones inside the package though... maybe it's us?

I don't need to tell you that **social media is very addictive.** Depending on your age, you will be either one of those who say that social media is taking over our lives or one of those who hear it all the time... And in fact, **on average, each US adult spends 3.5 hours on social media each day.**

This means that social media has become a major factor in our lives, and, in turn, of the way we think.

How Social Media Isolates You

3.5 hours a day are by far more than adults spend with their friends every day. And because of the nature of social media, that time may actually be subtracted from time spent with family members too. I will give you a little time lapse to show it to you.

Let's take a family from the lower or middle to lower class. Let's place this family, for example, at the beginning of the 20th Century. What would they be doing in the evenings? In many cases, you would have them all round a fire, some knitting, some reading if they had the knowledge and money (books did cost a lot at the time), and, in many cases, they were listening to stories, or, in some cases, reading was actually done aloud, for everybody (that was typical in centuries past in the middle class).

In any case, people sharing personal experiences, with stories etc., was the norm. You did have the night out at the local "public place" (whichever it was, according to the country, a pub, bar, etc.) for men, but when at home, nights were spent listening to older people (including parents, relatives and, especially, grandparents).

That went on till the television became very popular. It depends on the country, but in some cases, the TV only made it into almost everybody's home only in the 60s and 70s, and even then, most families only watched one program at night, often the news, at least at first.

But let's tele-transport our family into the 1980s of example. What would they be doing? To start with, in what were first basically extended families, even if not living under the same roof, by 1980, evenings were a "nuclear family" affair. Parents and children watching TV in their home, grandparents maybe just a few hundred yards away, but in front of their television…

Stories from the old days? Forget them. Some families kept their tradition, especially rural ones. But even then, these "old fashioned nights" were limited to summer nights when friends got together, maybe in the open air. In urban settings, this tradition virtually died out. If parents went out, once in a blue moon, they mostly went to places where children didn't fit in… So, going out became even rarer, as you would need a babysitter or, if you are lucky, a friendly relative.

But here notice how the circle is closing around the individual, especially around young people growing up in the different eras. A child grew up listening to the stories of his/her parents, relatives, grandparents, and family friends or neighbors once.

Then, by 1980, most children would grow up mostly talking to their nuclear family, but no longer at night (the time for fun and storytelling, not for practical talk, like "how did school go?"). At night, most of the time was either disconnected to the family, it was the TV that set the conversation (mostly done by short comments, soon followed by "ssssssh!").

Wind forward to recent years and watch! Most of the time is spent either watching TV, or on social media, and in other cases, there is also the time spent on video games to add. **How much do you interact with others around you, physical people, when on social media?** Very little. Maybe you will talk a bit more in front of television. When playing video games, isolation is complete.

Those 3.5 hours spent on social media is time subtracted from real, in person and meaningful relationships. This alone should convince you to cut down on them.

But remember that *one of the key strategies of mind manipulation is isolating the victim!*

When you are reading something on, for example "InstaTram", can your mother, brother, friend tell you if it's a lie? How often do you check with "real" people? In most times, very little, if not at all.

You can see how the ability to pass on an idea, a piece of information etc. without the risk of being contradicted is the perfect advantage for liars and mind manipulators. But you can say, "Ah, there you are, but I can check with my online friends!" True, but those online, many times, will not be able to give you a different point of view from yours... Why?

Internet and Social Media Bubbles

Have you heard of social media bubbles? Basically, *social media (and search engines) use algorithms to "suggest" what you should buy, what you should read, what you should watch and who you should be "friends" with.* Have you ever noticed how eager social media is to show you "suggested friends"? You will always find them in very visible positions on the page. And "making friends" (following etc.) is very easy...

But how do they select them? **They select people that the algorithm identifies as "similar to you".** This may look and sound innocent enough when "similar to you" means people who like cats, like you, or gardening, like me... But when it comes to deep rooted ideological ideas, like extremist groups, things become a bit more sinister.

And guess what? It's very easy for these algorithms to identify and match these ideas. In fact, you will be aware of the **radicalization of extremist groups on social media...**

Because you see, the **"group of people who think the same as you on a topic" is called a "bubble",** and some bubbles are fairly open (the gardening "bubble"), but the more the bubble is based on extremist views, the more the bubble itself becomes isolated (from other bubbles, or groups of people).

This is a very dangerous phenomenon, as you may well be aware of. These people basically end up in "sects" that have no contact with other groups of people online. Not only, but because they all think the same, **the bubble becomes a sounding chamber for their extremist ideas.** If you could look inside one of these bubbles, you would see that the people who shout the loudest, who are more extreme (even violent) are those who get most "likes" ... This is *positive reinforcement of negative, extremist, intolerant and even violent behavior.*

And this makes them radicalized and very dangerous...

This is a very topical issue as you will know. It shows without a shadow of a doubt that *social media is capable of mind manipulating large masses, and can even push them to accomplish criminal acts on a vast scale.*

We know that *terrorist organizations use social media to radicalize and spur of action.* The question is, however, "Why do they use social media for this?" and the answer is, "Social media are powerful mind manipulators; they have perfect structures for it, and they create the perfect environments for it."

From a historical and psychological point of view, we had not yet solved the problem of mind manipulation on TV when a new, more isolating, more powerful system of mind manipulation came along: social media.

Social Media and Behaviorism

Let's start with a question: take any social media you know, what is the system of "rewards" it has? How important is it? How frequent and repeated is it?

...

The answer is of course that the "heart", "star", "thumbs up" is a system of rewards, and that it has become a very, very sought-after reward by social media users. It is repeated frequently too... That's perfect behaviorism, and that is mind conditioning at its purest state.

So, how many "likes" did your post get yesterday? Well, think that every like is positive reinforcement, think that you are like a mouse in a Skinner box... Maybe those "hearts", "stars" and "thumbs up" have a more sinister function than their lovely looks want us to believe...

We have already said this, but it's worth remembering that social media also has negative reinforcement, and that mainly comes from other users: *you get negative reinforcement when you say something unpopular.* Negative reinforcement comes in the form of negative (sometimes rude, offensive, and even threatening) comments from other users.

Now, imagine being inside an extremist bubble. What do you think is the effect of positive and negative reinforcement on the social medium used?

...

You will imagine that in an extremist bubble, the negative reinforcement can be very unpleasant indeed. So, this works to totally root out any form of dissent, any idea of "contradiction", and, in many cases, even of fact checking.

In a more open field, like in a public forum, there may be a different effect. But hold on, if you are a reasonable, polite person who likes to discuss things nicely, your reinforcement is *neutral.* If you are a vulgar and violent person, you actually can take part in mass mind conditioning.

So, *social media gives the power of negative reinforcement only to people who are aggressive, negative, vulgar, violent, and rude.* Whole, polite, and gentle people have no effect at all.

Where do you think this reinforcement will lead? There is a *huge*, *structural problem with social media.* The only solution is to change the very structure of these media platforms, and there are countries that are trying to do this. How?

Well, algorithms! Oddly enough, they can be used to promote positive messages. The EU is now discussing a law that would force social media to use an algorithm where insults, threats, and even fake news would be "depreciated", sent down the "feed". That would discourage negative behavior, as being aggressive would mean being "less visible" not "more visible" as is nowadays.

And, as we mentioned it, we might as well talk about fake news on social media.

Fake News on Social Media

Fake news is one of the latest additions to mass mind manipulation. There are now "fake news factories", basically "marketing agencies" of ill repute that systematically and scientifically produce fake news, so that people's minds can be manipulated. There is basically a big business of fake news.

The problem is when the fake news is circulated in a bubble; you see, there you have no one who is willing to fact check it, and even if you did, you would never dare say it is fake, because of the massive negative reinforcement you would get.

Oddly enough, people who receive fake news in bubbles are very often the same who then accuse others of "being asleep" or "being under mind control". It's a very interesting phenomenon. But in their bubbles, they're repeatedly being told that they're being given access to some repressed truth, while at the same time they are being fed loads of lies.

But don't get me wrong. There can be repressed news. Actually, there has always been repressed news in the modern world. A whole war between the then USSR and Japan was fought and the whole war was kept secret by both!

The point is that *you need to check the reliability of the news you see*. True, journalists are no longer good at that. They too spread fake news. They too have ideological bias. But to claim to be different only to do worse is somewhat ironic, no?

The vast majority of fake news comes from social media. But it is true that even mainstream TV channels and magazines and newspapers have increased their own publication of fake news in recent years.

How to Fact Check Fake News

"Fine, so fake news is everywhere," you can say, "but how can we free ourselves from it?" Good question, and this is one of the steps you will need to take to **choose your information sources correctly.** We touched on this topic when we were talking about the television, remember? We basically agreed that you would not jump from TV to internet immediately because the internet is as, if not more treacherous than the television itself!

To start with, and this is my main piece of advice, **keep your standards super mega ultra-high**. People are often very "forgiving" with internet news outlets. You see, you don't end up in an extremist bubble not having noticed some fake news in it, or from the main information sources within it. You end up in there having *forgiven* the source for some fake news... Maybe (mostly) because they were convenient...

"Well, it's not true (I suspect), but I'll repost it all the same," (consciously) and, "because it suits my world view, the version of the story that's convenient for me," (more or less subconsciously) are not simple "carelessness", they are self-delusional and they're self-damaging! These are the thoughts that open up the door to mind manipulation and mind manipulators.

Can you imagine a better victim than one who is willing to believe a lie? That's why you must make sure that you keep your standards super high.

So, what happens if a source that has been reliable but then passes on some fake news? This does happen by mistake, there is a sea of fake news nowadays... **Check the willingness to correct it, and say, "We got it wrong, this is the real news".** This is now even portrayed as "weak", (it's a way to undermine reliable sources), but in fact it's a basic standard, an ethical obligation... It was once called *"errata corrige"* and reputable newspapers and magazines always had them, with, "In the last issue we said [xyz] but in fact it is ["so and such"]. We're sorry about it."

So, **the hallmark of a reliable information source is the willingness to admit its own mistakes.** The exact opposite of what mind manipulators would like you to believe...

Primary and Secondary Sources

Sorry, I have been watching a famous historian's lectures these days... But if you studied history you know what I am talking about. When I studied the language of newspapers at university, in a course that was very much centered on language manipulation, I was amazed to find out that most articles are massive cut and paste jobs...

You see, articles "report" and "spin" news. Reporting means taking the information from somewhere (it used to be Reuters, the AP, etc., now a famous plastic blue bird online is a major source of "information" for newspapers). They "report" interviews, and very often they "report" even other newspaper articles.

For a historian, **news outlets of most sorts are "secondary" sources.** To say it in a simple and memorable way, they're mostly "second if not third hand". They are not the original source, which, instead, historians call **"primary sources".**

For example, a newspaper tells you about a new law (say a stimulus check to be topical). Fine, that is not the original source of the information, is it? So, which one is the original source? The text of the law itself.

But this text has first passed through a government representative who has explained it to the media. Then this explanation has been written down and re-adapted by a journalist. Finally, an editor has checked it and even changed it to make it appear in the light of what the newspaper, site etc. actually wants it to have. By this time, you know how many spins the actual law has had? How many opinions have been added to it?

Odd that when you are writing an essay at school, they ask you to "quote" your sources and then reference them, but professionals only quote (misquote, even) opinions of experts or celebrities, hardly ever actually quote important sources and they almost never reference them.

I watch a news site on a famous platform. This is not a mainstream site, though it is quite in depth. In the description, it *links all the primary sources of the show.* I find this very reliable. Even written articles, blogs etc. often have links... Very often, however, these links are only a marketing tool. Why? They just link you to other pages of the same blog or newspaper!

Instead, trust those that, if they're talking about a law, for example, or some data, they link to the original source of the data. It's easy to write "200 billion birds fly over NY every year," without any actual source to prove it, isn't it? So, if you say it, at least if it's the main point of your article, do me a favor and give me the link to the statistics, the study, the data that proves to me you are not lying...

This is again, expecting that your source *does not claim to be the authority, but gives you a link to a true, reliable, and impartial source.*

It will take you a little to get into the habit of double-checking sources, but then, little by little, you will be able to select a set of reliable sources that are good for you. Once you have established which sources and news outlets you can trust, you will only need to do this sporadically, for extra safety or in case you have any doubts about maybe a particular item.

Could I suggest reliable news and information sources to you? Yes, of course I could. But I won't do it, because you need to trust yourself first, not me, I can only show you the way, tell you the tricks. Actually, beware of suggestions unless they come from trusted people you actually know or at least you really trust. Even then, double check the reliability of the channel, newspaper etc. Even trusted friends can make mistakes. Even trusted friends can be fooled by manipulating media…

Look for Consistency

We all change our mind every now and then. But if you are a person in the public eye, if you are an "influencer" of any sort, when you change your mind on a topic you need to say it, and explain why.

Instead, many outlets, channels, and influencers follow a double false line:

- They never admit they're wrong (especially if confronted).

- They change their mind often and they don't tell you they made a mistake, or they changed their mind "because" … xyz …

You see how the two things are contradictory? Also note the pattern of mind changing:

- *Do they change their mind every time general opinion changes, or worse, every time someone "higher up the influencer hierarchy" (a politician, some big, vested interest) changes tune?* In this case, "their minds are being changed for them", and in any case they are not reliable.

- *Do they change their opinions according to their convenience, or what is convenient for their narrative, or view?* These too are unreliable.

Finally, **expect consistency**; if they state a rule is valid for someone, a group of people, or an idea, then it must be valid for everybody, all groups of people and all ideas. Even major TV channels have "double standards". If someone on their political side does something wrong, they are very lenient, sometimes they try not to mention it altogether, or put a justifying spin on it.

When politicians "on the other side" do something wrong (or not even that!) they get on the moral high ground and pontificate or sometimes they become aggressive.

Instead…

Expect Correctness

Everybody has an ideological bias. There is no escaping it. Your values will always inform what you say, how you say it and how you interpret things. And you too may be looking for a news or information source with a specific perspective.

The fact is that *reliable information sources, news outlets etc. are correct even with people who oppose their views.* It's fine to disagree, but do they treat adversaries with respect? If they slander them, if they tell you lies about them, if they attack them "under the belt", for example with personal attacks, insults, insinuations on their personal life, comments on their looks etc. Then, for sure, they are not reliable.

Respecting adversaries does not mean liking them, nor agreeing with them. It means, for example, that if they are talking about a person, they give that person a chance to reply. Talking behind people's backs is not acceptable in real life. It does not become acceptable if you do it on social media either.

If they are news outlets, do they invite the people they criticize to speak their mind if possible? Do they stick to facts and actions when criticizing, or do they bring in a "character assassination" strategy?

Do they overstate things, or do they keep a level head?

Expecting correctness from those who give us information is simply expecting a basic professional standard. It's like expecting professional behavior from a medical doctor… You see, *manipulators have only to gain if we lower our standards;* in fact, they willingly encourage us to do…

Very correct informers instead will want you to raise the standards you expect, even from themselves. At least they should not encourage you to lower them. There's a guy I used to watch on an online channel, he always closed (he still does) his shows with, "Never trust what you read and only half of what you see."

Why do I like it? It's reminding us to keep our critical minds active and keep very high standards. I won't make any "endorsement" to individual channels for ethical reasons; I am here to tell you that *you need to choose your sources well but also independently.* So, I can't be the first to go against it, can I? But his channel is an investigative journalism channel that deals a lot with mind manipulation and disinformation…

Finally, *how can you trust a channel, influencer, newspaper etc. which is not correct with adversaries to be correct with you?* This is a question that many people should ask themselves when they see their favorite vlogger attack their "enemies" ruthlessly and dishonestly… Most cheer them up… Instead, they should think, "Hold on, this guy passes on information to me. How in the world could I ever trust him?"

Understand Bias

Everybody has his or her ideological bias. Whenever we relate to something, we take a perspective on it. In fact, I would not even trust someone who told me, "What I say is completely unbiased," especially when it comes to hot topics, politics, world views, etc. Of course, no commercial could ever claim to be "impartial".

But *many influencers, channels, news outlets etc. claim to be free from bias, while in reality they are not.* That is a form of mind manipulation. You see, we bestow a lot of trust on "impartial people" like judges. And I have found fake accounts on social media that pretend to be "impartial" while passing sentences on a topic. Then you look at their timeline and you find that they always condemn what a particular side does, never the other side…

Imagine two drinks, two similar drinks, for example. Let's call them "Code" and "Popsy". Fine, they are not new but very popular and there are many people discussing them online – there is a lot at stake if you win or lose this match on which is better.

Would you put it past a CEO or marketing manager to hire a social media marketing company with false accounts that go round changing people's opinions? And which is the best position to change people's minds? One of perceived (faked) impartiality. Don't need to put it past CEOs. Many political organizations use these strategies all over the world. And that is manipulation on a massive scale.

But *bias does not necessarily need to be a negative trait.*

I'll give you an example. I love gardening, remember? But I actually like organic gardening. So, I will look for information on organic gardening sites, channels, look for organic gardening books and magazines etc. These all have an ideological perspective. They do not like chemical products.

You see, the fact is that these *sources are honest about their bias, and they treat adversaries with respect.* This is the bottom line. John cannot be unbiased about, for example, Human Rights, he will always advocate for them, but he says he does, fine? How about those who instead are against Human Rights, but they don't admit they are? They of course already start with an incorrect, dishonest and **hidden bias**. And it's very hard to get them to admit bias.

Very often, when you corner these people, rather than admitting their bias they block you and move onto the next discussion. Discussion in which they will pretend they have not learned anything from you... For them, blocking you and starting afresh is a "reset". They are interested in influencing you and those who read the thread, but even if you prove it to them that they're wrong, it just takes them a "click" and they can pretend you didn't say anything. And they will pretend!

Like me, like most people, you will want to find information sources with views that agree with yours. And you will find them. But **don't start from the premise that because their views are similar to yours, they will not want to manipulate you**... If they are not correct, open, or their facts don't check out, if they don't admit their mistakes, if they don't respect adversaries and so forth, they are not reliable.

It also happens that **groups of manipulators collect followers in one area and then slowly lead them to another.** So, they for example attract people with one political view and slowly lead them to another political position. So... When you find someone with a view like yours online, do not assume that this is their actual view, the view they hold away from the keyboard. They may well be "fishing" in your group to lead you slowly to their actual and real views.

I know, it all sounds so treacherous and in fact it is. For this very reason you need to **expect fair play.** It's easy to get caught up in cheering sprees for your team... But that can work against you in the end.

True, social media is a far more sinister world than people think. You have algorithms that control your freedom without you even noticing it, bubbles where you become isolated, you have marketing agencies that have accounts ready to manipulate you, you have groups of people who pretend they like you and then slowly convince you of what they actually believe etc...

Fake Accounts

... and then you have fake accounts. Loads of them! And even here things are much more complicated than most people know. There are different types of fake accounts.

Bots are **automated accounts**; these are literally remote-controlled accounts, often small, and they have a "crowd" function. They manipulate people's perception of reality by making it appear that a post, an idea etc., is popular or not. This is their main function.

They also have other functions, like amplifying a post's views (often with fake news or a very partial) and pushing it up the "charts" (trends, timelines, anyway to make posts more visible).

Sometimes these also post a little comment, or at times, they are automated so that they post a given sentence. They are used for "storms"; they all post the same hashtag or sentence in a short time, so people think it's popular.

It's the high tech and modern version of astroturfing!

How do they do it? They repost, they put "thumbs up" or "stars" etc. As simple as that. And there are apps that do it automatically on your profile. You just need to enter a handle or profile name in "always re-tweet this profile". And every post will automatically be re-posted, or liked if you want... Do you know how many "influencers" (including politicians and pop stars) use them?

But how many are these? In July 2018 Twitter shut down a whopping 70 million accounts (!!!) because they were clearly fake! This time I had to mention the company, sorry...

How can you recognize bots? It's fairly easy:

- **They are usually small accounts with few followers.**

- **They have a very limited scope;** they only deal with one topic, or one celebrity, or one politician... They basically are a "one trick pony".

- **They often have long numbers in their handles** (at the end of the name, on Twitter, there are 8 numbers in most bots).

- **The profiles are not convincing on closer scrutiny;** you will notice that they have no "real personality", that they are limited in their description etc.

- **They interact very little.**

Avoid these, or block them altogether. There is basically no point in talking to bots.

Then there are **sock puppets.** These are far more problematic. They are **anonymous accounts managed by someone behind the scenes.** These **look real, even with pretend pictures of themselves, clear interactions, and a "personality".**

You will see that the face pic is always then fake, like bought from a stock image company. Alternatively, they use catchy images. **They often have one or a series of symbols next to their profile** (frogs, flags, even ducklings can work as "codes"; they use them to recognize each other online; it's like saying, "I belong to this group").

They will interact a lot; actually, these are in some cases those that launch the big posts. In a marketing or propaganda team, basically you have a group of people. Each has many accounts, and none has the actual name of the user. They can have dozens each! The accounts these manage themselves are sock puppets. So, instead of a politician saying something bad against the adversary (which would look bad!) they get a sock puppet to do it, so it looks like some real person did it.

And then they pay for bots to like the post, to re-post it and make it look like many people think the same. Then, other, smaller sock puppets, will come in to defend the main post. These have very typical argumentative strategies...

They use things like **kettle logic** (they don't respond to a critic, but they relaunch with another point), or **red herrings** (if you say something, they will point out something different, like "squirrel!" so that you go down that path) ...

Why do they do that? Because if you go and argue against the posts of the sock puppets you play in their hands... The post will gain visibility according to the likes, the re-posts but also the interactions, the "comments". It does not matter if these are positive or negative. And how many people actually read the comments? And what do people do when there are loads of comments? They skim through quickly... And if they see the sock puppets' supportive replies they will think that (1) many people actually do back up the head post; (2) they actually have real points to back it up. Both are fake!

Sock puppets often have many followers; and sock puppets of the same group always follow each other. They too are easy to recognize to the experienced eye, but for many people they look real.

Sock puppets are often those profiles that "shift opinion"; so, they will follow you, ask for your friendship etc. because you are in a "target group". Then as "friends", they will start passing (dis)information to you that will slowly change your mind, and you will get new "friends" that follow the same information etc. until you end up in a bubble and where you have not even realized that your opinion has changed. And by then, you are surrounded with people who think the same and reinforce that (almost always false) belief, and no one contradicts them.

They basically "absorb people into a bubble" a bit like amoebas… It's a horrible image; but it's actually like this.

So, careful with sock puppets.

Don't trust accounts that don't actually show their real face.

"Catalogue faces" as I call them, are easy to recognize. They look professional, they often have a neutral background, they just look like models… And you will never find a second picture of them in the whole profile or timeline.

But how about people who want to have a social media account but don't want to show their faces?

Some people have found a way out. In the end, you only need to receive information from a small, trusted group of accounts. So, there are groups that privately share pictures, even regularly, so they all know who they are behind the scenes, and they all know they are real people, but they keep their anonymity in front of the whole wide world.

As you can see, people are very creative indeed, and ingenuity can save you a lot of problems…

What's in a Word? The Language of Social Media

We already touched on this point, once more, in the chapter on television. But I think it's worth reminding a few points and maybe looking into them in more depth. *We use language to shape our ideas, and language manipulation is manipulation of ideas.* One of the reasons why feminists around the world are particular about "taking control of language that describes them" is that if the language is freed from patriarchy, thought is freed from patriarchy.

We also looked at **doublespeak**, a concept developed by George Orwell in *1984*. But there are more Orwellian traits on social media than this. There's a clear *Animal Farm* realization... Do you remember the dogs and the sheep in *Animal Farm?* Sock puppets and bots have very similar functions to these two allegorical animals respectively.

And these often push *intimidating language.* Note that they start slowly, by making simple, low level insults "acceptable". Like calling somebody "stupid" online is an insult, but the word is not too strong... So, they use it for some time till it is accepted, then they move on to a slightly stronger word...

You can see what this has led to: outright life threats and the like. *They slowly push the boundaries of what language is acceptable, and of what ideas (discrimination etc.) are acceptable...* By the time they have reached their objective, all sorts of horrible things have been normalized.

It's a Nazi technique, to be correct. But Orwell gave us a clear picture of how it can be used in less dramatic, tragic, and extremist contexts. So, *never trust any account, channel, blog, news source that is trying to "normalize" offensive language, insults, offensive ideas, personal attacks etc.* These are just the dogs and sheep of some propaganda machine.

P.S.: There are many propaganda machines at work on social media at the moment. Many political leaders have their own, as do political parties but also corporations, groups with hidden intents and many more...

Avoid "screamers and shouters". To start with, theirs is a show! They're not "outraged" by what they are talking about. They're just using an old *marketing technique.* You may remember TV salespeople who shouted all through their TV sale? They did it to pretend to care... It worked. People got a headache, but they bought their products.

Now many political, social and cultural commentators are shouting like deranged people all the time. *They want you to think that they care deeply about what they say. It's a lie.* Any professional notices how this is just an act. You can see how they decide which trigger to use to start their *performance,* and how they artificially wind themselves up...

You will also notice that some of them (especially those more into their careers) do it for virtually anything. It's like screaming mad over a drop of spilt water. *Many become excessive, even grotesque with their fake rage.* That's explained by their role. They are radicalizing people. And the more people follow them, the more they need to take them into a radical position. But these people, to be kept under the manipulation. Need more and more, stronger and stronger "doses" and reinforcements...

I compared it to a drug on purpose. Now, new waves and generations of disinformers come onto the social media stage regularly. They start more moderately and then they become extreme, even clownish... Till they are no longer useful, and they get replaced.

So, *careful with any signs, any tendency to convince you by just shouting, by winding you up instead of by explaining things clearly to you*. Think about it this way, *in the end, the job of an informer, journalist, newsreader, commentator etc. is not to use you as their emotional punch bag, is it? It is to inform you correctly, clearly and with a level head.*

People take exams about things they feel very deeply! I did... I never shouted my ideas at a professor... I doubt I would have passed. So why shout at an audience if not to hit their emotional response, but switch off their brains?

We have already talked about it. But please, keep it well in mind.

You want to get *ideas and opinions expressed in an honest, clear, and commensurate way. It's their job to be calm, not yours to be the emotional valve of their (fake) anger... A professional should be able to report even the most dramatic news in a fairly calm and collected way.*

It does happen every now and then that even the calmest and most collected person loses control. It happens especially in debates where the speakers are heavily pitched against each other, where the presenter does not get them to respect the rules or where the rules are not clear (or don't exist).

But careful; people who do it regularly and especially willingly are trying to manipulate you.

The Two Faces of Social Media

I shall close this chapter with the image of the Roman God Ianus, always depicted with a head with two faces... Social media offers you a wide range of sources. Some are wonderful. I listen to debates, speeches, documentaries, plays, etc. while I am writing... I watch the films I choose at night... I also find lots of data I need, and research papers... books!

And social media can be used to share these. But *avoid using social media as the platforms where you shape your ideas.* Reading a linked article from a reputable source is cool. But making up your mind according to what accounts scream is allowing someone behind a monitor to manipulate your mind. Ah, by the way, think of them as "accounts" and not people... It really helps.

So, again, *you need to take charge of your life, of which sources you allow to pass information and ideas on to you and which not, which types of arguments and language you allow into your world and which not, which type of influencers you listen to (professional or not) and which not.*

Now you know what to look for and what to avoid. You should feel empowered now. You can defend yourself from social media mind manipulation!

We are now coming towards the end of this book, and we have seen lots of strategies to defend yourself from manipulation of many types, online, on TV, face-to-face etc. The next chapter though will be full of light and hope. Why? Because we will look at the "aftercare" in a way, but also at the positive path you can start as soon as you decide to fight off manipulation...

Do you remember when we talked about Behaviorism that it "wires" your brain so that you respond in a certain way? Do you remember that we said that you can "rewire" your brain too? That's exactly what you are going to learn next...

Chapter 12 – Deconditioning and Rewiring Your Brain and Mind

Do you remember that time you had the flu, and you went straight back to work or school as soon as the main symptoms subsided? Or I'll give you a more pleasant example... Do you remember that mad weekend when you didn't even get home and went straight to school or work? In both cases, how did you feel?

Of course, you felt "groggy", "under the weather", "hazed" etc. Why? Your body and your mind were simply not ready to function at their best. Ok, the flu has gone, but everything we do to our mind and our body leaves traces, symptoms, and consequences long after the actual problem has ended.

In mental terms, the consequences can last for a very long time, even months, years, or a lifetime. Just think about how long it takes people to recover from a breakup... So, this leads us straight into the major point: it takes time to heal.

Understand Natural Time Cycles

"Time is the best healer," they say, and it's true in many ways. The main issue is that we live in a society that encourages us to "rush". Being fast, coming first, beating the competition etc. are all encouraged by this modern world, especially at school and in the workplace. This is the reason why most people have, at some stage, gone to work without having recovered fully.

When you see a medical doctor, s/he will sign you off work for longer than the actual symptoms of the complaint you have. But for mind conditioning symptoms, and many other problems that we don't see doctors about, you need to use a bit of DIY, don't you?

So, you will need to understand how our body and our mind work along *natural cycles of time.*

It makes a huge difference if you take an afternoon off or a full day off, doesn't it? If you take half a day off, you don't get half as well, half as relaxed, half as refreshed or half as re-energized as if you take a full day off. You receive fewer and lesser benefits in proportion...

Why? Because our mind and body need a full 24 hours to let go of some thoughts or problems completely. Imagine you are trying to push a big jelly blob out of a skylight... If you only do it partially, it will slide back into your room, won't it? This is why we have relapses. It's like we leave the "blob" in question (a virus, a mental problem, an ailment) half in and half out... It does not bother us too much at this stage, but as soon as you turn your back on it, it comes back.

Now I will give you another example. Think about when you have an argument, or someone says something that upsets you... If the person comes back to you after 5 minutes, are you ready to talk normally? The answer is, of course, "no"! The same applies to children when they have a tantrum. What happens if you bring up the topic again in a matter of minutes? They will start the tantrum again...

This is again because of a **natural unit of time in our mind,** one of the smallest we can use at this time. **The minimum time it takes us to calm down is 20 minutes.** So, if someone gets worked up, give her or him 20 minutes (be generous) to calm down...

Note that the media never gives people 20 minutes to unwind when they are trying to spur you up. Infuriating news follows each other fast and clashes come in quick succession...

So, we already have **two units of time to use: 24 hours and 20 minutes.** You need 24 full hours to get over any sort of significant damage. You need 20 minutes to calm yourself down.

Then again, if 20 minutes is one third of an hour, 8 hours is one third of a day… And you need *8 hours to sleep.* The 8-hour pattern is far more important than people think. We find it in nature, and even mind manipulation studies are aware of it. Most psychedelic "trips" have a basic 8-hour pattern too. Our mind is capable of "switching between realities" in this period of time.

All strong hallucinogenics have a basic 8-hour effect duration (it changes, it goes up and down, some have a very long "after", but this time crops up again and again as the basic duration). What can we understand from it? We can think that *it takes our Consciousness 8 hours to absorb a deep and significant experience.* It looks like we actually need a "change" for 8 hours a day, in fact.

Sleep and dreams have become central to many healing and self-development, even de-conditioning practices. We now understand them in a different way from the past. The practice of *lucid dreaming* can in fact have amazing results when it comes to rewiring the brain, deconditioning the mind and even expanding our Consciousness.

Then again, there is the *lunar cycle, 27 days.* For a full recovery from traumatic experiences, you will need a full *moon phase.* This has been studied in different contexts, including in molecular biology. Gabrielle Andreatta and Kristin Tessmar-Raible carried out an in-depth study on this, which appeared in the *Journal of Molecular Biology* on May 29, 2020 with the beautiful title 'The Still Dark Side of the Moon: Molecular Mechanisms of Lunar-Controlled Rhythms and Clocks'.

It gives us an insight into how deeply lunar cycles time deep processes in many species, and, though most is still to find out, they conclude that "the accumulated data from different species underline the importance and likely complexity of the processes involved." This is only to show that it has deep biological connections, but how about with our mind?

It appears that *moon phases have an impact on our sleep* for example. According to Csilla Zita Turányi et al. their research shows that "the results are consistent with a recent report and the widely held belief that sleep characteristics may be associated with the full moon", as stated in 'Association Between Lunar Phases and Sleep Characteristics', which was published in *Sleep Medicine, Vol.15, Issue 11,* November 2014.

In any case, if you want a practical suggestion, use this long cycle for important healing processes. For example, if you really need a big holiday, take 27 days off if you can (I know most people can't – but I am talking about that "big break" some people may need after serious crises, stress etc.).

If you need to get into a new habit, take 27 days of repeating it, and it will become natural to you…

Then of course, we have *seasons*; these have strong emotional connections, each season has its own mood, its "feeling" and its identity. Sometimes, we identify a whole experience with a season. For example, summer love stories take up the whole essence of a whole season.

Finally, of course, at least on the Human time scale, we have *years*. A full revolution of the Earth around the Sun is a very important time, both symbolically and psychologically. But don't take New Year's Eve as "the day everything changes". That's just a date like many others.

Understanding natural time and cycles means allowing each problem the necessary time scale to heal. You will not get over serious mind conditioning in a day or a week; even less when we talk about the "after effects". However, you can get over the direct influence of an advertisement in 20 minutes.

You see how it works? Serious damage will take more time. In fact, you will not get over the cumulative effects of commercials in one day, nor a week from when you stop watching them...

Neuroplasticity: The Brain and Its "Wiring"

There are different theories on how the mind and brain work. The mind is not as easy to "break into its individual components" and describe as the brain. Mind you, there is still a lot we do not understand about the brain, but...

The cells inside our brain are called neurons. You may have seen them. They look a bit like a spider or octopus, or a strange sea creature with a bulging head (called "soma") and then long tentacles (called "axons"). These axons have many terminals, a bit like the branches of trees, or the fingers on our hands.

These terminals get in touch with the terminals of other neurons forming **synapses** (or **synapsis** in the singular form). Basically, the axon terminals look a bit like receptacles (like shower heads, some may say). These face each other and exchange **electrochemical signals.**

It is with these electrochemical signals that neurons exchange information. On a mental level, this is **the way ideas travel inside the brain. The more a synapse is used, the stronger it and the axon becomes.** This is why we find it easy to recall ideas, names, dates etc. that we use very often: the path is clear, large, and fully in use.

The more a synapse is abandoned, the more it and the axon become weak and ineffective. We may look at the process like branches drying up in a tree... Little by little that "through path" disappears... This is how we forget things.

If a stimulus is followed by something unpleasant, we will avoid that synapse in our mind, so that path will wither. If it is followed by pleasure, we will "walk that path" more willingly and often and that synapse will strengthen.

You already knew this principle, but now you also understand it in a physical, neurological sense and dimension. It's like building up muscles or letting them go flaccid on many levels.

The ability of the brain of producing these links, and developing new pathways is called **neuroplasticity.**

Drugs and Brain Wiring

There is something few people are willing to say about psychedelic drugs. There are now many studies that say that psychedelics don't just "cause visions and hallucinations"; they actually have the power to develop many of those synapses we talked about, including in areas of the brain that we normally use little, or pathways that we usually do not follow.

We could say that they "make us think in new ways". Many people even within the creative, inventive, innovative and business world now use "microdosing" to help them think better. They take very small doses of substances like LSD; these do not make them "trip", but they still have the effect of facilitating new connections in the brain.

This is now a well known factor. As Dr. Lily Aleksandrova says in 'Food for Thought: Can Psychedelics Boost Brain Growth Factor Levels?', we now know that "research shows that BDNF (brain-derived neurotrophic factor) can help rewire and overwrite stubborn neutral pathways by creating new connections that facilitate more flexible and adaptive thoughts and behaviors. Psychedelics appear to tap into this mechanism."

Of course, I am not suggesting that you take psychedelics. But this explains why the CIA and others used them a lot in mind conditioning. Maybe, however, with studies coming in now, these psychedelics may be used in the near future by professionals to help the rewiring of manipulated minds. The progress in the health benefits of cannabis moves in that direction, and it appears that Ayahuasca in particular has impressive qualities in freeing up the brain from mind conditioning. For example, it makes people stop taking other, addictive drugs. And Ayahuasca assisted therapy for addiction is being developed by scientists as we speak.

It's in fact not a new type of therapy, already in 2013, its effects were being tested, and Gerald Thomas et al. from the Center of Addictions Research of British Columbia, Canada, state that "this form of Ayahuasca-assisted therapy appears to be associated with statistically significant improvements," and that "alcohol, tobacco, and cocaine use declined".

Can You Rewire Your Brain without Psychedelic Drugs?

"Shall I be waiting till these new therapies are available to everybody," you may wonder? The answer is a resounding no! Of course, you can still rewire your brain without "chemical assistance". Things will happen more slowly, and you will need a lot of determination to do this, but if you follow some guidelines, you will succeed. Many people have.

We already touched upon it, remember? We talked about vaping in depth for example.

Replacement therapy is in fact a way of rewiring your brain. And we have already seen that. But at the same time, you will want to *aid the neuroplasticity of your brain while you use the replacement therapy or other methods.*

And there are many tips I can give you to help you along the way.

Choose the Best Timing

Like with all therapies, if you start it at a good time, you are much more likely to succeed. Imagine starting to rewire your brain when you know you will have lots of practical problems...

You see, when we have to solve lots of problems, our brain tends to go down those paths it knows better because it can be quick. This means that, *in a problem-solving mode, you will tend to strengthen already developed synapses, and not develop new ones*.

There is more; think about when you have emotional problems, can you think properly?

...

I agree with you! You can't. There is no denying that when your heart is suffering, your brain does not

256

work correctly. There are many physical explanations for it. Chemists will tell you that when we suffer, we produce substances and hormones that prevent us from thinking properly.

Other perspectives may simply tell you that when the neurons in your heart (or guts) are strained, they override those in your brain. A more holistic and mentalist approach will say that the heart and mind are two sides of the same experiential process, and that when one is strong, (e.g., the heart) the other allows it to express itself till it can rest and be peaceful.

It doesn't matter which approach you prefer; they all say the same thing: you can't think properly if your heart is suffering… or if your guts are in the grip of fear. We'll talk more about fear soon.

Choose a time when you are at peace, when you don't expect problems. Start at the weekend, not on Monday. Start when you are off work or off school. Start when you retire. Start when you have a stable relationship. Start when you move to a better home… Start in summer or spring, not winter (unless you live in Australia, New Zealand, South Africa etc., of course!)

Don't Let Fear Dominate You

Let's go to your guts… did you know that *we have more than 100 million nerve cells in our guts*? It's another brain. We actually have a few brains around our body. And this is *the brain that sprints into action when we are in danger*.

If you meet a lion in the savannah, you need to change your thinking mode from analytical or emotional to… "emergency". So, the brain in our head takes a back seat, and the one in our guts takes over. We go into a "safety mode", which, of course, does not allow us to think properly.

There is a reason why mind manipulators at high levels (I am thinking about politicians, here, especially tyrants and autocrats) keep talking about danger, risk and instill fear. Media that only cause fear in readers and viewers do the same. They talk to your guts. *If you feel fear, you cannot think rationally.*

But how can you practically achieve this?

- *Avoid (eliminate, if you can) all media that talk and shout about dangers and fear.*

- *Don't worry if you don't succeed. You can try again, and again.*

- *Take time off news and media every day.*

- *Take up calming and relaxing activities.*

- *Avoid violent noise and noisy places.*

- *Keep in touch with Nature.*

We will find the last one, keeping in touch with Nature is useful for quite a few points in rewiring the brain. As for noisy places, even if we get used to them, they provide a continuous stimulus for your gut neurons. They give a "background impression" and that is one of fear and danger.

Now, onto talking about taking "time off" from the news and media...

Prepare for Bed

Are you one of those who watch the news last thing at night? If you are, you will have to change that... Think about, for example, when you go to bed and suddenly a problem comes to your mind... what happens?

...

For most people, this will keep them awake, maybe for an extra 20 minutes, maybe an hour... maybe all night! Now, what happens to your dreams if you watch a horror movie at night?

...

It depends on the movie, true, and on how far you are used to them. But let's take really scary movies and more susceptible people. Why? Because the symptoms are more visible. It does not mean that other people don't have the same reaction. Their brain works in the same way... Only because they are more used to these stimuli it reacts less...

Ok, you know what I am hinting at... Many people literally have nightmares. But hold on... let me ask you a trick question: does our brain work when we sleep as well?

...

Of course it does! And it does wire and rewire even during those 8 hours... And it's not little...

It takes a minimum of 40 minutes to unwind before going to sleep. In this time:

- *Only watch, read, talk about positive and pleasant things.*

- *Get yourself comfortable.*

- *Take relaxing herbal teas, like chamomile.*

- *Use relaxing smells, like lavender incense sticks etc.*

- *Listen to relaxing music.*

- *Don't think about problems and work.*

Preparing for bed is very important indeed. You see, you **recover your mental and emotional strength**, and this will make a huge difference the day after, when you will need willpower, stamina, and strength to keep rewiring your brain.

What's more, is having 8 to 10 hours of calm makes rewiring the brain itself much easier and faster. It's like starting again the day after from a neutral or almost neutral state, if not positive, instead of a negative one. You are already "closer to your aim" when you wake up in the morning!

If you can spend even more time doing this, even better. I spend all nights, from when I have supper onwards unwinding from the day... Which leads me to the next tip...

Find a "Switch off Time"

On top of preparing for bed itself, you need a moment when you say, "This is my 'me' time," and not "work time" or "problem time". Work worries often linger on into the evening, then at night. And that weakens you, and makes rewiring far more difficult.

But to do this effectively, you can't just say, "Fine, it's all over with work," in most cases. You need to:

- **Unwind**

- **Get it off your chest**

This is why the "how did the day go" question and conversation with families, flatmates, friends etc. questions are very important. And it must be followed by good, honest and liberating conversations. I know, listening to other people's problems when you get back from work or school can be hard. But think about it this way: you are, in a way, counseling each other. You let your significant others get it off their chest, and they allow you to do the same. Just take turns and after a few times you'll have a well-oiled routine.

Try to **close this routine with positive points**. Follow the format "these things went wrong and upset me, then these things went well". You can even have a little **ritual to mark the transition into the "me time".** Many people have a glass of wine (red is far better, it relaxes, white wine makes you nervous) to unwind. It could be a good ritual. Tea, a walk in the park etc.... All will do, even singing a song!

I would suggest getting all these things off your chest, again, before the evening meal. **Keep the evening meal as a starting moment for "me time".** If you can earlier, even better. You see, the importance of **eating with a positive mindset (at least once a day) has amazing effects on your mind, brain, and mood.** It's, to start with, major positive reinforcement.

But eating also has very primordial, visceral, ancestral links. Doing this correctly at least once a day is very invigorating, it allows you to find a positive connection with your nature, even at the most basic levels. One of the problems of modern society is that we spend little time dealing with food. We spend too little cooking, eating, planning meals, etc. This is one of the most important relationships we have with our nature.

Eating a microwaved meal in front of the television in a hurry is not healthy at all. It allows all sorts of influences on you (while the food is giving your positive reinforcement). Instead, if you do it in a peaceful, natural way, **the positive reinforcement of the meal will go to your own nature, and feeling confident about your nature is key to rewiring.**

Rewiring Is Like Training

Think of rewiring as training, like for sports. Can you train equally well when you are feeling tired? After you have had a massive night out? When your mind is somewhere else? When your diet is not appropriate? Of course you can't. This is why **you need to have the right conditions to rewire your brain correctly and set yourself up to succeed.**

But there is more... Have you ever trained for some sport? How would you describe the progress you made? I don't mean, "How much progress did you make?" I mean how was it at first? Did it go in phases? Did your training change over time?

...

I think you will say what most people say... It was hard at first, then it got easier, then it became "second nature to you". And these, roughly are the same phases for everybody and for rewiring the brain too.

- **The first few days are the hardest.**

- **Success is slow at first.**

- **In this phase, you are "learning the ropes", the basics.**

- **After a couple of weeks, it becomes "challenging but feasible".** It still takes considerable effort, but at this stage you feel that you can manage it.

- *Results become more visible and faster.*

- *At this stage, you learn from your mistakes and you also work out what's best for you.*

- *Progress accelerates, and you tailor the training (rewiring) to your personal needs.*

- *Then, after a long time, it becomes "customary", "usual", "easy" and second nature.*

- *At this stage though, your progress actually slows down.*

- *What you are doing at this stage is mainly consolidating your achievements.*

This is what will happen, and remember that the consolidation phase is very important indeed. Reaching the top of a mountain once does not mean you can reach it again... But if you consolidate your climbing skills, you will do it again and again. Things become feasible even when you are not 100% if you consolidate your skills.

Mind Your Diet

Your brain consumes 20% of all the energy your body uses every day. That's an awful lot! And it does not even move a single muscle! But it's not just a matter of quantity... It's a matter of quality too.

It is now ascertained that a poor, unhealthy diet (especially early on in life) is responsible for decreased intelligence scores, even later in life. And it's now ascertained that *your diet and your lifestyle affect your neuroplasticity.* A study on elderly people with cognitive issues by Christy Phillips, finds out that there are three main "modifiable lifestyle factors" that affect neuroplasticity: "physical activity, cognitive engagement and diet."

No need to say the typical US diet is poison. We said it already. In particular, you need to *cut down on animal fats and sugar.* These literally slow down mental processes and even cause lots of health problems that will then affect our brain.

The ideal would be to have *a healthy, organic, varied plant-based lifestyle*. It does not mean that you have to become vegan, but that the bulk of your diet should be healthy, plant derived and rich in carbohydrates and vitamins, fatty acids and minerals. Of the carbohydrates you take, don't forget fiber.

Many of the "substances that oil our brain" are contained in vegetables, like vitamins, long chain omega-3 fatty acids, folic acid etc. A Mediterranean diet, as you know, would be ideal, and it's super tasty too!

Keep Your Brain Fit!

One of the three factors that make your brain more plastic, so more easily rewired, is ***"cognitive engagement"***. You know when people look at old writers, scientists etc., maybe in their 90s and they say, "How lucid s/he still is!" Yes, people who use their brain regularly will keep it fit, and it will keep healthy into their old age. It's as simple as that.

The problem is that people think that watching the news is using your brain, you now know it's definitely not: it's in a passive mode. And we cannot train by being passive. So...

- ***Read a lot.***

- ***Listen to good music.***

- ***Go to the theater.***

- ***Have cultural conversations with friends, even debates if you can.***

- ***Take on an artistic hobby (gardening included!)***

- *In short, engage your mind in active (!!!) mental activities each day, for at least a few hours a day.*

Even learning a new language, going to evening classes etc. are very good, like doing crosswords and so forth. You got the gist!

Mens Sana in Corpore Sano

I haven't had far too much to drink… *Mens sana in corpore sano* is a famous Latin saying which means "a healthy body in a healthy mind". And it's true! **We need to look at our body as a whole.** If your body is not working well, it will divert energy from mental activities to see to other problems. This is why when you have a temperature or when you are in pain you cannot think well.

Choose a Positive Setting for Your Rewiring

Re-wiring requires a positive, peaceful and healthy setting. Of course, this is not always possible. If you want to do a little rewiring exercise when you are queuing at the post office, fine. But if you have a decently long session in mind, say 15 or more minutes, choose a good place to do it. It will work far better.

- *Avoid places linked with work or negative activities or memories.* Your office is not the best place.

- *If possible, choose a place which is natural or with a window on a natural, green space.*

- *Choose a quiet place.*

- *Prepare the place of how you want.* People like to use perfumed candles or sticks, or even just sprinkle a few drops of some relaxing essential oils, like lavender, sandal etc. If you want, *put on low volume relaxing music and have ambient lighting.* This will really help you rewire your brain.

- *Tell people you don't want to be disturbed.*

- *Switch off all distractions: TV, radio, computer or that terrible cellphone!*

- *Make sure light, humidity and temperature are fine.*

- *Avoid artificial light!*

On the last point we need to say a bit more. Artificial light keeps you awake and alert; it does not allow you to relax. To start with, lower lights 40 minutes before bed. But in these sessions, if you can, use natural light or candlelight.

Do Meditation

Meditation is by far the best way to prepare your mind for rewiring. It's also, as we have seen, an outstanding way of de-conditioning your mind, and freeing yourself from manipulation.

A quiet mind stops the repetitive and even "automated" synaptic firing that reinforce those paths induced by manipulation. A meditative mind is the quietest we can have. Even quieter than when we sleep in fact!

"But meditation is hard," I can hear some of you say… Not really… There are many ways of meditating, you don't need to sit in the lotus position to do it. Actually, the lotus position is only for experienced meditators.

You can meditate when you walk in a park or on the beach. You can meditate at home, standing upright, sitting comfortably or laying down. The key to meditation is just to switch off that rational, talkative mind, that voice in our head we keep hearing…

To do it, the best way is to concentrate on your breath. Just breathe in slowly through your nose, hold your breath in for a little while, like a second, you should not feel uncomfortable with it. Then breathe out slowly. Focus on it till you hear no more "words in your head".

If you learn to belly breathe (or re-learn to belly breathe, as when we are children, we do it all the time, just watch a baby), even better. And if it does not work the first time, don't worry; try again. You don't get fired if you don't succeed!

Use Music to Rewire Your Brain

Of course, music too can put our mind in a peaceful state and make it "open to rewiring". Even more, *listening to pleasant music while rewiring is a form of positive reinforcement.* But while doing the exercises, you need to listen to "the music your brain likes, not you!"

No heavy metal, death metal, punk, rock or other high energy music while you are rewiring. But you can treat yourself to Metallica *after* you have done the exercise as positive reinforcement. The problem is that *some music waves soothe the brain into receiving information, others distract it.* High energy music distracts you.

While you are doing the exercises:

- *Prefer slow peaceful music, with maximum one beat per second.*

- *Prefer music with real, natural instruments.*

- *Classical music (especially Baroque) is believed to be good.*

- *Meditation music is excellent.*

But avoid binaural sounds. There are a lot of "binaural meditation music" tracks online. Just don't! The problem is that they can cause more damage than good. The reason is that it is almost impossible to time the binaural sound to the other track. And if it's not perfectly timed, it has a negative effect.

Talking About Exercises

"But hold on," you're thinking, "you keep talking about exercises, but you haven't given us a single one!" OMG you called me out! Ok, then, just because you have, I'm going to give you a full chapter of exercises!

Chapter 13 – Exercises to Rewire Your Brain

Are you ready for some practical exercises? Don't worry; you won't build up a sweat. You can do most of the activities in this chapter in the comfort of your home. But sometimes I will ask you to go out. Contact with Nature has amazing effects, as you know. One thing though I need to remind you of before we start: *keep it positive! The rewiring, like replacement therapy, can only use positive reinforcement, never negative!*

So, on your marks, get set, go!

Belly Breathing

Let's start with a basic exercise. This will not in itself rewire your brain, but if you learn it, many other exercises and activities will become easier and more effective. There's something strange about the way we breathe... When we are children, we belly breathe, just like singers, athletes etc. No one knows why but at some stage, we start pushing our chest out to fill our lungs instead of pushing the diaphragm down and belly out (belly breathing, in fact).

Nevertheless, when we sleep, we revert into what appears to be the natural way of breathing: belly breathing. Belly breathing has a few major advantages:

- *You breathe more air.*

- *You oxygenate your brain better.*

- *You give your heart a slow rhythm.*

- *It is ideal for a meditative and relaxed mood.*

Let's try. First, breathe in normally. The only thing I will ask you to do is focus on your breath and your lungs. What happens to it? You "suck it in" with your nose, then you push out your chest (even with discomfort at times) and fill your lungs.

Now, focus on the bottom of your lungs, where your bowels start. Now breathe in through your nose, but this time, push the air down, towards the bottom of your lungs. Your belly will push, allowing your lungs to extend downward.

It may take a few trials, but once you remember how to do it, that's it.

Draw Your Dreams

What did you want to become when you were a child? What were your childhood dreams?

Visualizing is an excellent way of rewiring the brain. But I will ask you more in this exercise… I will ask you to go back to "before" the mind manipulation started, and using your memory, "graft your future self on your past self".

Get a nice box of crayons, a big white coloring paper, take time off all sorts of engagement and get drawing! It does not matter if you are a new Leonardo or just a scribbler. Put colors (positive ones) in your dreams, and bathe in the beauty of your childhood dreams.

When you do this, focus on the great pleasure you get from this activity. And at the end, pause for a second to enjoy the happiness this exercise has given you.

Smell Flowers

Does it look and sound simple? Well, it is! Our modern world uses the sense of smell to condition us, but it actually discourages proper understanding and active use of our sense of smell. Instead, building "perfumed" pathways in our brain is a way of building long lasting synapses.

I say flowers, but it can be any smell you like. Re-engage with your sense of smell, and use it as positive reinforcement. When you smell something, rather than trying to describe it, just focus on its "presence" and on the feelings it arises in you.

Get used to making positive links with positive, especially natural smells in your life. This can become a major asset when you want to shift your mind from an unwanted brain path to one you wish to encourage and develop.

Flip Your Conditioned Behaviors

Take a piece of paper, make it a big one. Draw a line in the middle and on the left-hand side, write down all the behaviors you feel are being manipulated in you. Use bullet points.

Take a walk... Do something positive and fun. Come back, and for each negative behavior put a comparable positive one on the other side. For example: "I eat too many sweets," on one side with "I will eat more fruit," on the other side. Yes, sugar is addictive... Or if you want, "I buy too many useless things," can change into "I will give my useless junk away to charity every week."

Try to turn the negative into positive. Now, if you can't "counter" each negative behavior at first, don't worry. Go back to it later...

What do you have now? You basically have a "roadmap" to change all the behaviors that have been induced into your personality. Shopping changed to helping others is actually a very useful switch. People often become shopaholics for many reasons, but having a social activity, like talking to the charity people etc., as a replacement is quite good.

Mind Your Language

Every time you say something, you make it a "deeper part of your personality". This is how people develop *idiolects* (the individual languages of each person), how people develop those words and phrases that they use all the time.

That's fine, but may I ask, are there any phrases and words you use a lot and you do not like?

Fine, make a list, and then write an alternative phrase of words next to each. Cross out the one you don't want to use, and underline, highlight or circle the ones you want to use.

Now it is time to remember.... Every time you are about to use a crossed-out expression, try to replace it...

Use Positive Language

I had a friend who always started his sentences with "no". He wasn't very successful, no need to say. He also had many confidence issues. You see, when you use negative language, you do two things with it:

- *You externalize it.*

- *You internalize it.*

So, start your sentences with "well" instead of no. When you disagree, do it with a positive opening ("I can see what you are saying, but..."); avoid "I hate", "I can't stand" etc.

Now, I wouldn't go so far as some sticklers do... You know, there are people who say that you should never utter anything negative... Of course it happens, of course people have to get it off their chest. I actually think that "not using negative expressions at all costs" can be counterproductive if people need to release tension, pain, suffering, worries etc....

But *changing your language to a positive one will make following positive in your mind much easier.* Think about words as road signs... The more road signs leading to a good thought you have, the more easily you will find it...

Use Positive Affirmations

Positive affirmations are a way of teaching your subconscious to be positive, and follow paths you set for it. It is one of the most powerful rewiring exercises we have.

Basically, what you need to have is one or more sentences with these qualities:

- *Positive affirmations are simple and clear.*

- *Positive affirmations are short.*

- *Positive affirmations express willpower.*

I will give you a few examples:

- "I will eat more fruit during the day."
- "I will be happier when I wake up in the morning."
- "I will smile more often."

Make them suitable to your aims, your plan etc. These are like the "good version of mind manipulation" in the sense that they work on the same level, the subconscious. But instead of making you do things someone else wants, *they teach your subconscious to recognize your real will.*

You will need to repeat them over and over again (like manipulators do). You will also need to say them when you are quiet, calm, and receptive. You can say them to yourself for a few minutes every day, maybe before going to bed. That, as you know, is a time when our mind is very "open to suggestions".

But another time in the day would be fine too if you wish. Once more, when queuing at the Post Office for example. Or driving instead of listening to music that plays negative lyrics. Those "dead moments" in the day are excellent to rewire your brain.

Repeat them slowly to yourself, with calm and peace. You can use music, like slow, meditative music, to give you a rhythm for them if you wish. This too, works very well.

Regardless, always try to remember to *connect the positive affirmations with positive reinforcement.* Something healthy, preferably.

You will see the results creeping in slowly after a couple of weeks. It may be earlier, it may be a tad later.

If I can be a bit insistent, do use positive affirmations in your rewiring; they work wonders.

Use Visualization

How do you want to change your life? Who do you want to become when you free yourself from mind manipulation? No – don't tell me! I want you to *picture it in your mind* instead!

And get used to it! Get used to visualizing your aims, your objectives, your dreams, your positive journeys. You should do it regularly, in a peaceful place. If you can go to a park or a beach. Otherwise, indoors will do too, but set up the room like we said for mediation.

Just close your eyes. If you can meditate, do it and add this level to the visualization. If you want to bring a radio with relaxing music, fine. But birds singing will do quite well. Sorry, we don't use radios any longer, I know, cell phones then! In any case, visualizing while meditating pushes the images deeper into your mind.

Use candles, naturally perfumed sticks etc., if you wish. Make sure you feel comfortable, and wear comfortable clothes. Take your time. Don't do this when you are in a hurry. Above all, make sure you are well hydrated. We think and visualize better when we are hydrated. It's like watercolors! Sorry, joke...

Ok, you can picture what you have in mind in front of you, or better still, you can put yourself in the middle of it.

You will notice that when you visualize, it's not like you are fully in control of the images. They tend to take on a "will of their own" and draw themselves. This is fine, but who is drawing them, then? There are many theories, and I will stick to a simple and easily accepted one: it's your subconscious and your unconscious that are painting the pictures in front of you...

Note here, that people who have suffered heavy mind manipulation will often see negative, unpleasant and even frightening pictures coming from their subconscious. But have no worries about this and above all *don't take them seriously!* Make fun of them! It's the only way to get rid of them.

If your mind is fairly in control, you can easily push negative images aside. But after string manipulation, if you push them aside but you respond emotionally (you are scared, disgusted etc.,) they will come back. That is the manipulation trying to force itself onto you.

So, if you can be neutral, fine. But even better, laugh at them. That literally breaks up the pathways in your brain that lead to the manipulated goal... A trick that victims of strong mind manipulation have invented is to turn them into stupid cartoons! You can do it fairly easily.

A cartoon is not taken seriously to start with, and then you can make something stupid happen and you laugh at it!

Anyway, this is only in serious cases... In most cases, you will simply be able to visualize beautiful things, and that will rewire your brain to positive ideas, pathways, thoughts, aims and behaviors...

Laugh!

This is not actually an exercise... But laugh a lot! Watch comedy, tell jokes, don't take yourself too seriously... Did you notice what we said just now? When you laugh, you "ease the synapses related to that topic", this means that you ease the pathways to certain thoughts.

It has told you that deconditioning could be fun...
Well, it should be fun, actually, even better, the
more fun it is, the better it works!

Conclusion

Isn't this a raving mad world we live in? When I was a child, I thought mind conditioning was something belonging to Japanese cartoons. I grew up to find out that not only is it possible... It is, if you forgive me the phrase, in full swing!

I grew up to learn psychology, and in my studies, I became interested in dark psychology... Finding out that experiments on how to condition minds started centuries ago was only the beginning... Coming into the de-classified documents in CIA experiments, their cruelty, their range, the weaponization of mind manipulation, to then use it against innocent citizens... - well, that was a massive shock.

But even more, seeing that low level, but all-pervasive types of mind manipulation that uses the very language we speak and write, the newspapers, movies, television and even social media to keep us under control... - well, that actually promoted me to write this book.

And I hope I have helped you.

I have avoided personal opinions in this book. It's a very "sensitive" topic already; I have cracked a few jokes, used metaphors and tried to make your reading pleasant – but correct and informative. But my opinions have stayed out of it. Till now. Now we reach the end of this journey, I will express a personal thought: in my view, *mind manipulation is a crime against Human Rights*. Why? It goes against the very *Article 1 of the Universal Declaration of Human Rights:*

> *"All human beings are born free and equal in dignity and rights. They are endowed with reason and conscience and should act towards one another in a spirit of brotherhood."*

What do I see in it? I see that conscience belongs to us; it belongs to the individual and no one else. Trying to change my, your, or anybody else's Conscience against my, your, their will, is in fact a crime against this very first article.

We need to *take back control of our Consciousness and conscience.* Only when that is guaranteed will we really make inroads against mind manipulation. So far, it remains a "crime that society tolerates", like rape, torture and murder were in the past...

I am sorry I have had to take you into the bowels of hell with the studies and experiments (and outright crimes) done to manipulate people's minds. But it was necessary for you to know about it and then fight against it.

I hope I have helped you.

I am glad, on the other hand that you have learned all the theory and psychology that is behind this appalling practice. And I'm glad that you **now have the means to counter and fight mind manipulation with confidence.**

It is not an easy battle, but remember, it must be a positive one, even a funny one! **The more you enjoy yourself, the more you are happy with your life, the easier it is to get out of mind manipulation.** You can now see the light at the end of the tunnel...

In a way, the journey out of mind manipulation reminds me a bit of Dante's *Divine Comedy*. It's a journey to hell and then out of it, into heaven... And when the poet gets out of hell, or gets out of purgatory, or even at the end of the whole poem, there is always the same word: "stars".

He comes out of the darkness of hell "to see again the stars" ... We are living through dark times in terms of mind manipulation... But if I hope I have done something, well, I hope I have shown you a path out of this "dark forest" and that now, after reading this book, you feel more confident. That you will so, because you have so many ideas and techniques to push back mind conditioning moving forward.

You even know how to rewire your brain, and become the person you have always wanted to be.

So, in a way, I trust that now you too, after having read this book, can finally see the stars… Never lose sight of them, and your path will get brighter and brighter. As for me, I hope we will meet again, maybe on the pages of another book, and for now…

Cheers to gaining better control of mind manipulation.

Reference Page

There is so much to say on this topic that I can't tell you all in a single book. But if you are a curious mind, and if you wish to find out more, here is a list of books you may wish to check out!

- ✔ Baum, W. M. (2017). *Understanding Behaviorism: Behavior, Culture, and Evolution* (3rd ed.). Wiley-Blackwell.
- ✔ Browne, J. (2020). *Understanding the Human Mind: Why we need thinking time*. Independently published.
- ✔ Faber, K. (2019). *Mental Toughness - Unleash the Power Within: How to Develop the Mindset of a Warrior, Defy the Odds, and Become Unstoppable at Everything You Do*. Cac Publishing LLC.
- ✔ Goleman, D. J. & Press, TH. (2020). *REWIRE YOUR BRAIN: Understanding the Science and Revolution of Neuroplasticity. Rewire Your Brain, Body, and Soul to Change Your Mind, Develop a ... and Control your Anxiety Disorder*. Independently published.
- ✔ Green, E. (2020). *Proven Psychological Manipulation Techniques: Guiltless Guide into the Psychology of How Cunning People Get What They Want. How to Play Secret Dark*

Games to Seize Control and Always Win. Modern Mind Media.

✔ Green, E. (2020a). *Dark Mind Control Techniques in NLP: The Secret Body of Knowledge in Psychology That Explores the Vulnerabilities of Being Human. Powerful Mindset, Language, Hypnosis, and Frame Control*. Modern Mind Media.

✔ Hollins, P. (2018). *Psychological Triggers: Human Nature, Irrationality, and Why We Do What We Do. The Hidden Influences Behind Our Actions, Thoughts, and Behaviors.* CreateSpace Independent Publishing Platform.

✔ Jones, M. D., & Flaxman, L. (2015). *Mind Wars: A History of Mind Control, Surveillance, and Social Engineering by the Government, Media, and Secret Societies* (First ed.). Weiser.

✔ Kahn, M. D. (2002). *Basic Freud* (1st ed.). Basic Books.

✔ Ph.D., C. B. (2015). *The Neurogenesis Diet and Lifestyle: Upgrade Your Brain, Upgrade Your Life* (1st ed.). Psyche Media.

✔ Ph.D., H. S. (2014). *The Power of Neuroplasticity* (1st ed.). CreateSpace Independent Publishing Platform.

✔ Ph.D., H. S. (2019). *Negative Self-Talk and How to Change It*. Park Avenue Press.

✔ S. (2017). *MK Ultra Dark Labs*. CreateSpace Independent Publishing Platform.

✔ Skinner, B. F. (1976). *About Behaviorism* (1st ed.). Vintage.

✔ Soh, J. (2019). *Mind Hacking: Unleash The Hidden Power Of Your Subconscious Mind & Achieve Anything That You Truly Desire!* Independently published.

✔ Winship, A. (2019). *Neuroplasticity: Exercises to Improve Cognitive Flexibility, Conquer Trauma and PTSD, Change Bad Habits, Eliminate Depression and So Much More!* Independently published.